WILL AMERICA GROW UP BEFORE IT GROWS OLD?

PETER G. PETERSON

WILL AMERICA GROW UP BEFORE IT GROWS OLD?

HOW THE COMING SOCIAL SECURITY CRISIS THREATENS YOU, YOUR FAMILY, AND YOUR COUNTRY

Random House

New York

Library of Congress Cataloging-in-Publication Data
Peterson, Peter G.
Will America grow up before it grows old?/Peter G. Peterson.
p. cm.
Includes index.
ISBN 0-679-45256-7
1. Entitlement spending—United States. 2. Debts, Public—United
States. 3. Budget deficits—United States. I. Title.
HJ7537.P48 1996
336.73—dc20 96-21492

Random House website address: http://www.randomhouse.com/
Printed in the United States of America on acid-free paper
2 4 6 8 9 7 5 3

For my wife, Joan Ganz Cooney,
the "Mother" of Big Bird,
and my tireless sounding board for
longer than she may care to remember.

Acknowledgments

This book has dealt with debts, and I would be remiss if I did not say a few words about my own debt to the many people who have helped me through the arduous process of writing it.

Jason Epstein, a friend and legendary editor at Random House, put his heart, soul, and prodigious intellect into this project—commenting on new drafts as soon as he received them, questioning every assumption, urging me to fix small problems and large ones, making numerous constructive suggestions about points of history and economics, and line editing my sometimes convoluted prose. He championed this project from the beginning, and for that I am deeply grateful. I would also like to thank Harry Evans, President and Publisher at Random House, as well as the many other people at Random House who helped, including Jason's brilliant assistant, Joy de Menil.

This book began as an idea for an article in the *Atlantic Monthly,* and indeed, some of the material first appeared in that magazine. I benefitted greatly from the support, enthusi-

asm, and advice of the *Atlantic*'s editor-in-chief, Bill Whitworth, and his able colleague Jack Beatty, as well as the magazine's chairman, Mort Zuckerman.

From the rough outline to the published page, I received much valuable assistance from Neil Howe and Richard Jackson. Neil has worked with me through many of these relentlessly detailed, intellectually demanding, and endlessly iterative projects for fifteen years, and Richard has joined him for the last three. They are among the country's leading experts on issues relating to the federal budget, entitlement programs, intergenerational economics, and other matters that lie at the heart of this book's argument. They form an invaluable brain trust for me. Their contributions are found throughout this volume.

Many friends and experts read and reviewed the manuscript at various stages. They have offered new insights, suggested alternative formulations, called my attention to interesting statistics, and generally inspired me to see the project through. I would like to thank, in particular, Fred Bergsten, Marie Brenner, Ethan Harris, Craig Karpel, Bill McDonough, Cynthia McFadden, Cheryl Merser, Judy Miller, Peggy Noonan, Van Ooms, Diane Sawyer, Liz Smith, Tony Solomon, Ralph Willis, and Dan Yankelovich, and, of course, my colleagues at The Concord Coalition, Warren Rudman, Paul Tsongas, and Martha Phillips. I should also thank Warren Buffett for his insightful and delightful "Static Islanders" tale which he kindly permitted me to use.

Dan Burstein, Senior Advisor at The Blackstone Group, urged me to write this book at a time when I dreaded the thought of undertaking another. He persevered until I relented, and for that (I guess) I am grateful. He worked closely with me on organizing the material and reviewed and commented on innumerable drafts.

My assistants, Patricia Selden and Karen Boccio, deserve high praise and purple hearts for their devotion to the word

processing and other logistical tasks involved in this project. I also greatly appreciate the efforts of many other people who contributed to getting the job done, especially Nigel Holmes and Frank Pena.

Contents

WILL AMERICA GROW UP BEFORE IT GROWS OLD?

Introduction: Will America Grow Up Before It Grows Old?

A momentous question now looms over America's economic future. The way we face this question will likely have vast bottom-line consequences for your personal retirement. It may also determine whether your children will participate in the American Dream of rising affluence or whether our nation's wealth-producing engines will fail within your lifetime. I hope to show that the choice is up to you whether we become a nation in decline early in the next century or whether we continue to prosper.

The question is this: How will America prepare and pay for the growing dependency of our rapidly aging population? Graying means paying—paying more for public and private pensions, more for hospitals and doctors, more for nursing homes and other social services. Under our present system, we, as a nation, cannot begin to meet these costs when the huge Baby Boom generation begins turning sixty-five a mere fifteen years from now. So there is also a second question: What collective steps must we take *now* to assure that our obligations to aging Americans do not undermine our na-

tional prosperity, and what steps must we take as individuals to provide a secure retirement for ourselves? According to a recent poll, more Americans under the age of thirty-five believe in UFOs than believe they will ever receive Social Security. Unless we all begin now to provide for America's future and our own, time will prove them all too right.

The economic challenges posed by America's impending "age-wave" transformation have already forced their way into everyday conversation. News reports warn of projected trust-fund "bankruptcies" in Medicare and Social Security. Politicians talk about a widening but "untouchable" senior share of public-sector budgets. Surveys show that more and more American workers, including most young adults, are now pessimistic about ever receiving a dime in federal retirement benefits. Meanwhile, various crusades and plans to reform the large senior entitlement programs are surfacing—and for the first time, they are being taken seriously.

But so far, we have paid attention mostly to what's narrow and immediate and unavoidable: whether, for instance, to trim a bit off the rapid near-term growth of Medicare and Medicaid in order to balance the federal budget in the year 2002. Although this passes for a "strategic" and "visionary" debate on federal budget policy, it entirely ignores the real challenge: how to control the projected explosion in entitlement costs *after* 2002. Inevitably, voter cynicism ratchets up another notch.

One of the reasons why it's hard to come to grips with the challenge is that the sheer magnitude of the costs involved in sustaining our aging population defies conventional analysis. When a deficit projection is countable in the *billions,* we worry and take action. When the projection is countable in the *trillions*—as our retirement obligations are—we are more likely to collapse into denial and paralysis.

Despair, however, is no better than pride as an excuse for not facing up to our future. For we can, in fact, meet and over-

come our age-wave challenge. We can protect the security of our future retirees and we can also preserve and expand the American Dream for our children. We can revive the historic vitality of our economy. But we can do so only if we make an effort to understand our problem and start to solve it now before the crisis hits us full force a decade or two from now.

But how can this age-wave transformation be made real and palpable to Americans rather than a distant abstraction? When I speak in public and show charts that illustrate what the twenty-first century will really be like demographically, my audiences are shocked to learn that the soaring number of seniors will soon transform us into a "nation of Floridas," in which one out of five Americans will be sixty-five years old or older. They are sobered by the vast expense that this demographic shift will impose upon our system of universal retirement and health-care benefits—costs that we have absolutely no idea how to meet. I ask audiences to imagine, for example, how each working couple can possibly pay (through taxes) for the full cash and medical support of at least one retired senior citizen—in addition to all the other taxes this couple has to pay, to say nothing of the cost of helping their own parents!

The first step toward a better future is simply to confront, debate, and begin to "live" with the awesome reality of a much older America, one in which there may be fewer than two taxpaying workers to support each Social Security beneficiary. This new aging reality is not just narrowly economic. It will transform our work lives, our culture, our politics, our ethics, and our society from top to bottom.

Some listeners ask me, with understandable curiosity, how a businessman like me became so involved in the arcane policy world of senior entitlements. I tell them I became involved because I want today's rising generation to enjoy what my generation enjoyed during the so-called American High, the post–World War II years, when we took for granted that we

would find work, raise a family, and provide for our children's future as well as our own. "The ultimate test of a moral society," the German theologian Dietrich Bonhoeffer said, "is the kind of world it leaves to its children." So far, we are failing this test.

I am the son of Greek immigrants who arrived in this country penniless. When I was a child, I witnessed firsthand what can be accomplished by parents who dedicate themselves to posterity. For decades on end, my father, in Kearney, Nebraska, kept his small restaurant open twenty-four hours a day, 365 days a year. Every penny that didn't cover necessities or get plowed back into the business he set aside for his children's future. To him, being called a "big spender" was the ultimate insult. My situation was anything but unique. Many in my generation, and indeed throughout our history, have benefited from a similar ethic of sacrifice and endowment. But I wonder now if Americans of my generation—as parents or grandparents or opinion makers or public leaders—are imparting this ethic as forcefully as our parents imparted it to us. The risk we now run is that unless we begin again to save for the future, we will leave our economy without the savings we all need in order to prosper. Without savings, we can't create more productive jobs in the next century, and our children as well as our future retirees will suffer accordingly.

I have been on this mission for about a quarter of a century. In my first policy position, as President Nixon's Assistant for International Economic Affairs in 1971,* I encountered among American political leaders widespread denial that our global competitiveness was in decline. When I went to Washington, I was a recent alumnus of Bell and Howell, a photo-

---

* Since then, the U.S. economy has become far more engaged and integrated with a much larger, more open, and vastly more competitive world economy. Both U.S. imports and U.S. exports have doubled as a percentage of gross domestic product (GDP) since 1970.

graphic and business equipment company, and knew first-hand the increasing foreign competition from companies and countries that were investing far more than we were in plant, equipment, and research and development. But few policy makers cared: Back then, the wind was still at our back. It was not until the end of the 1970s that conventional wisdom finally recognized that we had become an undersaving and underinvesting economy and began looking for solutions.

In 1981, President Reagan proposed an answer: his supply-side gamble. I naively assumed that when the new GOP team said "supply side," they meant an increased supply of investment capital to create new businesses and new jobs. Instead, I was saddened to find that "supply side" meant spending and borrowing more than ever, not for the sake of building new factories but mainly for immediate consumption. Reagan's program was not really a supply-side, but a demand-side, philosophy, the same old Keynesianism only dressed up in new rhetoric—and on a much vaster scale. Beyond the spending increases (for defense) and tax cuts (for everybody and everything) was the belief that we could ignore the exploding cost of middle-class "entitlements" like Social Security and Medicare, that if we prayed really hard and kept the faith, the economy would grow fast enough to satisfy the myriad special interests that had staked out a legislated claim on future national income. The go-go hubris of simply assuming—rather than creating—rapid economic growth was no longer an affliction merely of liberal Democrats. The GOP approach to the eighties, as I wrote at the time, was to assume a make-believe sixties prosperity without bothering to produce it.

The supply-side hoax led me to my next foray into public policy. In 1982, along with five former Treasury Secretaries, I set up a group called the Bipartisan Budget Appeal. Composed of some five hundred distinguished Americans from both parties, this was, shall we say, a highly credentialed

group. We bought newspaper ads, cajoled Congress, and beat on administration doors—but to little avail. I soon concluded that our national consumption addiction was far too deep rooted to be cured by the "establishment." The problem, as I once heard former Governor Jerry Brown say at a New York dinner party, is that "there is no constituency for fiscal responsibility." He was right. Fiscal responsibility requires a knowledgeable and active public. With Senators Warren Rudman and Paul Tsongas, I therefore went on to found a grass-roots organization, The Concord Coalition, dedicated to bringing Americans at large into the debate.

It gradually became clear to me that the crux of America's undersaving, or, if you like, overconsumption, is the addiction to universal entitlements—welfare for all, in effect. I then embarked on a serious study of our entitlement system, much to the dismay of my best friends, to whom this preoccupation seemed like an obsession. This enabled me to complement my interest in eliminating the federal deficit with a growing understanding of the social and demographic forces responsible for this fiscal imbalance. My objective, as ever, was to learn how America could resume its historic levels of savings, investment, and productivity—the essential conditions for higher earnings, social cohesion, and ongoing prosperity.

At the risk of anticipating the pages that follow, let me briefly introduce the three major themes of this book. These themes—and their interactions—supply the structure of my argument.

- The first theme, *demography,* delivers a message that is unambiguous and unalterable: America will soon experience an unprecedented explosion in the number (both absolute and relative) of elderly. Over the next forty-five years, the number of people sixty-five and over will increase by roughly forty million—five to eight times faster than the

number of people between twenty and sixty-four. In 1950, there were just fourteen seniors for every one-hundred working-age adults; today there are twenty-one; by 2040, there will be at least thirty-seven. The abnormally large Baby Boom generation, born between 1946 and 1964, is now masking—but will soon accelerate—inexorable demographic forces pushing a historically young America into middle age and beyond.

- The second theme, *dependency,* translates these demographic factors, plus other trends such as earlier retirement and exploding health-care costs, into dollars. These dependency costs are the economic resources that workers will have to transfer in ever larger amounts to the retired elderly. Although some of the burden will fall on families, communities, and states, much of the cost will be borne by the federal budget. To learn how big the burden will be, try the following: The combined federal cost of Social Security and Medicare, expressed as a share of workers' taxable payroll, is officially projected to rise from the already burdensome 17 percent in 1995 to between 35 and 55 percent in 2040. And this does not include the many other costs—from nursing homes to civil service and military pensions—that are destined to grow along with the age wave, even if Congress never enacts another benefit expansion.

Obviously, an irresistible force will soon meet an immovable object as the Baby Boomers retire and demand the benefits which they have been promised and exert the political clout to collect them. The immovable object is tomorrow's taxpaying workers, who won't be able to pay anywhere near the tax rates required to honor these benefit promises and still enjoy a rising living standard.

A necessary element of any solution is already obvious: Retirees will have to adjust to smaller benefits, and on our current course the necessary adjustment will be far from

minor. To make matters worse, a large share of today's Boomers will be totally dependent on public benefits when they retire, for they will have very little, if any, savings of their own.

This brings us to our third theme.

- The only way to ease the tax burden on future workers, without radically cutting benefits for their elders, is to *increase thrift, the sine qua non of greater pretax productivity.* This means saving more of our current income and investing it in the tools and research and education that make workers more productive. Meanwhile, the only way to ease the pain of reduced benefits for future retirees is to increase their private sources of retirement income—that is, their net household wealth. Since the usual way to do this is to save more, we once again arrive at the same prescription: Those future retirees who can possibly afford to increase their savings should be encouraged or obliged to do so.

The vital role that higher savings plays in any solution to the age-wave challenge is underscored by the very meager savings performance of the U.S. economy. In recent decades, America has saved a smaller share of its net output than any other modern economy—on average, less than a third of the share in Japan or the newly industrializing Asian economies. Thrift was thus bound to be a critical issue for America in any case.

The coming age wave makes thrift doubly important—not only because our economy needs savings so that future wages can rise faster than the costs of supporting the elderly, but also because *the very dynamic of age dependency tends to undermine savings and investment* by imposing ever greater benefit costs that crowd investment spending out of public budgets and that increase the deficit—that is, *negative saving*

by government. This negative saving cancels out private saving and investment dollar for dollar. Another price we pay for encouraging future retirees to count on public benefits which the government has failed to fund is that these unrealistic promises *directly lower private-sector savings rates by discouraging families from saving as much as they otherwise might have.*

How big will deficits be in the next century? Consider that in the year 2030 the official estimate puts the *annual* combined operating deficit of Social Security and Medicare—that is, tax revenues minus outlays—at $1.7 trillion. As for total unfunded federal benefit liabilities, they are now $17 trillion—or about $170,000 of hidden debt per family. The $1.7 trillion annual deficit might be regarded as an indicator of our "macro" challenge: how to prevent benefit costs from crowding out private savings, and how instead to ensure that these savings are translated into productive investment and economic growth. The $17 trillion in accumulated obligations to today's workers and retirees is more an indicator of our "micro," or household, challenge: how to encourage one hundred million American families to save more of their current income rather than rely on benefits which (except for those dedicated to the poverty safety net) must sooner or later be cut well beneath today's levels.

The task at hand is daunting, but it need not test the outer limits of our ability to sacrifice, for what is now a vicious circle can become virtuous. If households save more, they will become less dependent on public benefits. If we trim back benefits, households will be encouraged to save still more. Meanwhile, higher rates of national savings, both public and private, will make productivity increases possible, which will mean more income per worker and more public revenues. This, in turn, will make the relative burden of any given level of public costs more bearable.

I will present in this book a reform program aimed at

bringing about just such a virtuous circle—a program that includes several direct public-spending cuts targeting benefits that are least effective and beneficiaries who are least in need. I will propose an "affluence test" that scales back on a highly progressive basis all federal benefits to all households above the median income; a higher eligibility age for Social Security and Medicare; and a package of health-care reforms that will introduce market discipline into our blank-check system of reimbursing doctors and hospitals.

But public savings alone will not close the gap. My program also emphasizes individual and family thrift. Following the lead of cutting-edge reformers around the world (from Australia to Chile), I will propose a mandatory defined-contribution retirement plan for working-age Americans. Eventually, the *funded* benefits of such personal and portable pensions will replace most of the *unfunded* promises currently offered by Social Security. I will also suggest changes in the tax code to encourage savings, as well as a national "savings crusade" to encourage still greater personal thrift. A higher rate of household savings will not only make possible greater productivity and provide greater retirement income, but it will also provide a better buffer against sudden job loss—as well as the means to improve career prospects by investing in one's own skills and education. In a fast-changing global economy, career security built upon abundant human investment—intellectual capital, really—must also be part of anyone's definition of a rising living standard.

The biggest obstacle to this or any other effective reform plan is not the sacrifice required. The biggest obstacle is procrastination in face of a challenge which, unlike Pearl Harbor, never quite demands our immediate attention but threatens our national security no less than an enemy attack and possibly far more.

Yes, when I confront apologists for the status quo with the ominous projections, they agree that we absolutely must re-

form entitlement programs. Yet when I talk to these experts again, the "reforms" become "adjustments." Then those "adjustments" become "options" that can be deferred from one year to the next.

But in a democracy, you can't blame only the experts, for the people themselves are ultimately responsible if they willfully deny the known facts. Consider what surveys tell us: A majority of all thirty- to fifty-year-old wage earners (a) believe Social Security won't be there for them, (b) are not participating in any meaningful pension plan, (c) have a personal savings rate (and a household net worth) hovering near zero, yet (d) expect to retire early with an ample standard of living. Even if most Americans know that they must change public policy as well as their own behavior, their actions, to quote Saint Augustine, say, "Lord, grant me chastity and continence, but not just yet."

Time is running out. If we procrastinate much longer, we will lose the opportunity to create the virtuous circle I described—and the age wave, when it hits just a few short years from now, will indeed require great and sudden sacrifices from workers and retirees alike.

For this time, if we continue to delay, we won't be able to muddle through. This time, the economy as a whole will be at stake. This time, millions upon millions of Americans will have neither adequate private pensions, nor adequate personal savings, nor adequate government benefits to support a decent retirement. The so-called golden years will turn to lead. Right now, America is passing through a wonderfully benign demographic period in which a huge crop of Baby Boom workers are swelling our tax receipts while a relatively small generation retires. But before we know it, these demographic forces will be thrown abruptly into reverse.

If the necessary reforms are implemented soon, they can be gradual and humane. I'm convinced that if Americans understand both the problem and the alternatives, they will accept

such timely reform as necessary, reasonable, desirable. But they need to know the truth, which is why, given the gap between public perceptions and the brute facts, there is no substitute for the heavy dose of reality this book tries to provide—nor for the kind of principled leadership that has always served us well in the past when informed and determined Americans have faced a crisis.

Will America, the ultimate here-and-now "youth" society, grow up and confront the long-term challenge of its own aging before it's too late? In this political season, it's hard to know which to regret more: the deafening oath of silence that prevents candidates from addressing our long-term economic challenge or the free-lunch, everyone-a-winner "solutions" that politicians like to give the voters. What's our instant cure du jour? A tariff hike? An interest-rate cut? A tax cut? A flat tax? Anything that's dramatic, immediate, and painless? We are indeed in danger of becoming a spoiled people to the extent that we hope to solve long-term problems—and our economic, retirement, and demographic challenges are all long term—with short-term fixes like these.

No one wants to see the day when millions of needy elderly Americans are faced with draconian cuts, and I don't mean the rhetorically draconian cuts the senior lobby now rails about. No one wants to see the day when millions of middle-income workers suddenly stranded with inadequate retirement incomes angrily ask their leaders, "Why weren't we told!" And most of all, no one wants to see our children confronting a far darker economic future than they expect and deserve—in the midst of a financial, political, and moral crisis that could have been avoided.

That is no choice at all.

1

"A Nation of Floridas"

Been to Florida lately? You may not realize it, but you have seen the future—America's future two decades from now.

The gray wave of senior citizens that fills Florida's streets, beaches, parks, hotels, shopping malls, hospitals, Social Security offices, and senior centers is, of course, an anomaly created by our long tradition of retiring to Florida. Nearly one in five Floridians is over sixty-five—a higher share than in any other state.

But early in the next century, Florida won't be exceptional. By 2025 at the latest, the proportion of all Americans who are elderly will be the same as the proportion in Florida today.[1] America, in effect, will become a nation of Floridas—and then keep aging. By 2040, one in four Americans may be over sixty-five.

When we consider the great demographic shift that will shape the American future, we are speaking not of a mere transition but of a genuine *transformation*. As Baby Boomers become Senior Boomers, they will bring changes—economic,

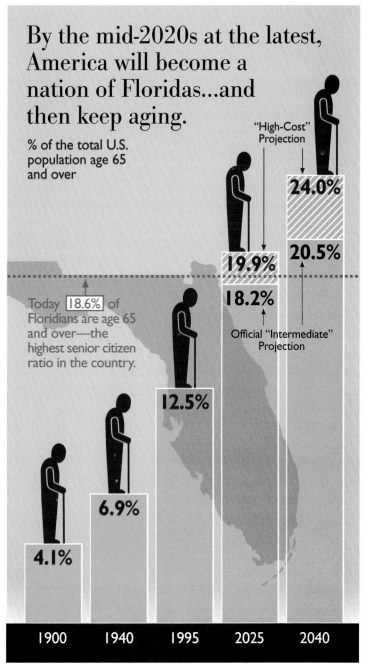

By the mid-2020s at the latest, America will become a nation of Floridas...and then keep aging.

% of the total U.S. population age 65 and over

"High-Cost" Projection

24.0%

20.5%

19.9%

18.2%

Today 18.6% of Floridians are age 65 and over—the highest senior citizen ratio in the country.

Official "Intermediate" Projection

12.5%

6.9%

4.1%

| 1900 | 1940 | 1995 | 2025 | 2040 |

SOURCE: Census Bureau (various years) and Social Security Administration (1995)

political, social, cultural, and ethical—that will transform American society.

This transformation will challenge the very core of our national psyche—which has always been predicated on fresh beginnings, childlike optimism, and aspiring new generations. How we cope with the cultural dimensions of this challenge I will leave to others—to sociologists, political scientists, historians, and philosophers. I am none of these. I am a businessman who has long participated in public debates over the political economy of rising living standards. What concerns me most about America's coming demographic transformation is simply this: On our present course, we can't afford it. To avoid steep economic decline, we must forsake our consumption and deficit habits and once again reshape ourselves as a savings-and-investment society.

Today's political struggle to balance our federal budget may seem daunting, but it is only a gentle warm-up for the marathon we must run over the next half century as we confront the $17 trillion in unfunded entitlement benefits that have been promised to federal beneficiaries above and beyond the value of their tax contributions.[2] To put the number in perspective, this $17 trillion liability is *five times* greater than the official public debt and *seven times* greater than the total current assets of the federal government.

To provide for the largest generation of seniors in history while simultaneously investing in education and opportunity for the youth of the twenty-first century, we must reject the prevailing entitlement ethic and return to what I shall call our endowment ethic, which generated America's high savings, rapid economic growth, and rising living standards in the past. "Endowment" implies stewardship—the acceptance of responsibility for the future of an institution. But given our current emphasis on individual self-fulfillment, we must emphasize that in addition to endowing the future of our nation and its institutions, we must now endow our in-

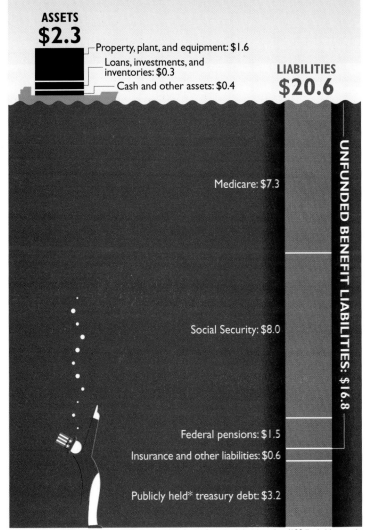

By normal accounting standards, the federal government is drowning in a sea of red ink.

Total **assets** and liabilities of the federal government, at end of FY 1995, in trillions of dollars

ASSETS
$2.3

Property, plant, and equipment: $1.6

Loans, investments, and inventories: $0.3

Cash and other assets: $0.4

LIABILITIES
$20.6

Medicare: $7.3

Social Security: $8.0

UNFUNDED BENEFIT LIABILITIES: $16.8

Federal pensions: $1.5

Insurance and other liabilities: $0.6

Publicly held* treasury debt: $3.2

SOURCE: Office of Management and Budget (1996); Social Security Administration (1996); A. Haeworth Robertson, *Social Security: What Every Taxpayer Should Know* (1992); and author's calculations
*Excludes debt held by the Federal Reserve System.

dividual futures and those of our children, because no one else is going to do it for us. What I am talking about is "self-endowment."

But before any of this can happen, the challenge of our aging population must become central to the political dialogue. Americans must discuss it, debate it, confront it, and prepare for it. Only then can we avoid not only our impossible financial future but also the prospect of "generational warfare" between working-age taxpayers and the exploding number of retirees whom they will be asked to support.

So far, we have failed to face up. We are a nation in denial, one of whose classic symptoms is exaggerating the pain required by the cure. The historian Livy said of his fellow Romans, "We can bear neither our ills nor their cures." Coping with the economic effects of an aging population calls for major policy changes that will affect all of us, but these changes need not mean unbearable sacrifice for ourselves and our families. Yes, middle- and upper-income elders must forgo part of their federal benefits, but benefits to low-income elders need not be cut; indeed, in the plan I shall propose, they could even be raised. Yes, most working Americans will have to save a few percent more of their income, but in return they will enjoy a secure old age. It's not pleasant to acknowledge that a generational chain letter has run its course—and that we'll now have to start paying our own way—but such an admission will only foreshadow hardship and crisis if we fail to act soon.

Let me be clear: Having just passed my seventieth birthday, I am thrilled by what modern science has done to extend longevity. I am also delighted that in recent years we have pioneered new and active retirement lifestyles for seniors. But to maintain anything approximating today's opportunities for seniors in the future—*and to do so without doing a massive injustice to younger people*—we must make major changes in a system of public entitlements that now passes

out huge windfalls regardless of need and, at the same time, substantially increase our meager level of private savings.

"Hope I die before I get old," sang the rock group The Who in their classic sixties anthem "My Generation." That statement, like so many slogans of the Baby Boomers' Peter Pan culture, was wishful thinking. The generation that once warned "Don't trust anyone over thirty" is now beginning to pass fifty!

The real question is: Will America grow up before it grows old? Will we make the needed transformation early, purposefully, and humanely—or procrastinate until delay exacts a huge price from those least able to afford it and confronts us with an economic and political crisis to which there is no longer a win-win solution?

2

Demographics Is Destiny

A demographic time bomb is now ticking, set to go off in 2008, when the first Baby Boomers turn sixty-two and start to collect Social Security. As the huge generation of Baby Boomers whose parents brought them into the world with such optimism begins to retire, they will expect the munificent array of entitlements that our government guaranteed (again with so much optimism) to every retiring American without anticipating the ever-growing length of retirement due to rising life expectancy or the ever-rising expectations of independence, affluence, health, and comfort in retirement. But consider who is expected to pay for this late-in-life consumption: the relatively small "bust" generation in whose productive capacity we have largely failed to invest. Neither the founders of Social Security sixty years ago nor the founders of Medicare thirty years ago imagined America's demographic shape as it will unfold over the next several decades.[1]

Ponder the following:

- With seventy-six million members, the Baby Boom generation, born from 1946 to 1964, is more than 50 percent larger than my so-called fortunate generation, born between the mid-1920s and mid-1940s. To get some idea of how much the number of seniors will grow by the time the youngest Baby Boomers are in their seventies, think of the entire population of California today plus that of all the New England states combined. Or think of it this way: By the year 2040, the number of seniors will be at least double what it is today.

- In 1900, only one in twenty-five Americans was over sixty-five. The vast majority were completely self-supporting or supported by their families. By 2040, between one out of every five and one out of every four Americans will be over sixty-five, the vast majority supported to some degree by government.

- In 1960, 5.1 taxpaying workers supported each Social Security beneficiary. Today, there are 3.3. By 2040, there will be no more than 2—and perhaps as few as 1.6. In effect, every young working couple, in addition to their other tax burdens, will have to pay the Social Security and Medicare benefits of at least one unknown retired "relative."

- The number of "young old," aged sixty-five to sixty-nine, is projected to double over the next half century, but the number of "old old," aged eighty-five and over, is projected to triple or quadruple—adding the equivalent of an entire New York City of over-eighty-five-year-olds to the population. Two-thirds of these old old will be women, and among these women, over four-fifths will be single, divorced, or widowed, the groups most likely to need extensive government assistance.

While the number of working-age adults will grow slowly, the number of elderly will skyrocket. By 2040 there will be roughly 40 million more senior citizens than today.

% growth in the population from 1995 to 2040, by age group

Age 65 and over

+129%
"High-Cost" Projection

+112%
Official "Intermediate" Projection

Age 20–64

+24%

Under age 20

+5%

SOURCE: Social Security Administration (1995)

There will be many fewer workers to support each Social Security beneficiary.

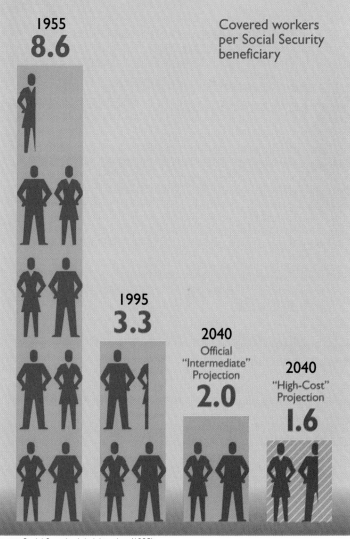

1955
8.6

Covered workers per Social Security beneficiary

1995
3.3

2040
Official "Intermediate" Projection
2.0

2040
"High-Cost" Projection
1.6

SOURCE: Social Security Administration (1995)

- In 1970, children under five outnumbered Americans aged eighty-five and over by twelve to one. By 2040, the number of old old will about equal the number of preschoolers, according to some forecasts. In 1970, there were just 1.4 million old-old Americans; by 2040, there could be 14.4 million—*ten* times as many.
- The extraordinary growth of the old-old population will add especially to federal health costs. This is because the average annual medical-care bill rises along a steep curve for older age groups. For hospital care, the ratio of public benefit spending on the old old relative to spending on the young old is 2 to 1; for nursing home care, it is over 20 to 1.[2] In other words, longer life spans add to health costs at an exponential, not just a linear, rate.
- In 2030, only about 15 percent of elderly Americans will be non-white. But about 25 percent of younger Americans will be non-white. This creates a potentially explosive situation in which the largely white senior Boomers will increasingly depend on overtaxed minority workers.
- To provide the same average number of years of retirement benefits in 2030 that were contemplated when Social Security was originally set up in the 1930s, the retirement age would have to be raised from sixty-five to seventy-four. But this projection—daunting as it is—assumes that future gains in longevity will slow as average life expectancy approaches the supposed "natural limit" to the human life span. Many experts now question whether such a limit really exists. Summing up recent research at the National Institute on Aging, demographer James Vaupel goes so far as to suggest that we are now on the threshold of "a new paradigm of aging" in which *average* life expectancy could reach one hundred or more.[3]

Of course, the United States is not the only country facing an age wave. Indeed, the age waves in most European coun-

America may eventually have as many "old old" aged 85 and over as preschoolers under age 5.

Millions of people, by age group

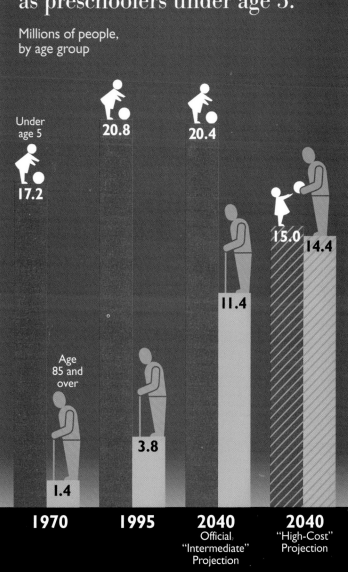

Under age 5

20.8

20.4

17.2

15.0

14.4

11.4

Age 85 and over

3.8

1.4

1970

1995

2040
Official "Intermediate" Projection

2040
"High-Cost" Projection

SOURCE: Social Security Administration (1995)

tries and Japan are approaching faster than ours and—at least to judge by official projections—will have an even worse impact on their public budgets and national economies.[4]

I used to believe that most other industrial countries enjoy long-term defenses that we lack and that the prognosis for reform was much more favorable. Unlike the United States, it seemed to me, most can actually "budget" their public spending on health care and so have much greater control over this potentially explosive dimension of senior dependency. Unlike the United States, most generally tax public benefits as they do any other income. And unlike the United States, most have fairly healthy household savings rates (generally well over 10 percent of disposable income, versus about 5 percent here) and so can absorb public-sector deficits much better than we can.

And as for AARP-type senior lobbying, it is far less formidable in Europe. I was also under the impression that other countries, facing similar demographics, were much more proactive in solving the aging problem. Australia has made employer pensions mandatory, boosting coverage from under 40 to nearly 90 percent of the workforce. Iceland has means-tested its social insurance system. Germany has enacted—and France, Sweden, Italy, and the United Kingdom are debating—increases in the retirement age.

But having recently attended conferences in Europe and elsewhere on the *global* fiscal issues associated with aging, and having spent time discussing these matters with European leaders from Italy, France, Germany, and the UK, I am no longer convinced the Europeans are in any better overall shape than we are.

Europe's problems manifest in different forms, to be sure. But they too have over-promised and under-funded entitlement programs on a massive scale. Indeed, as European experts quickly acknowledge, the unfunded liabilities of retirement programs in most European countries are signifi-

cantly greater as a proportion of GDP than ours.* Several countries also face annual government deficits considerably larger than ours, such as Italy's at 7.5 percent of GDP, compared to "only" 2 percent in Washington. What's more, if we think our politicians are spineless in facing up to the aging problem, Europe's coalition governments, fragile and shaky as they often are, are even less likely or able to take on tough long-term reforms.

Europe may lack a powerful counterpart to AARP, but its labor unions are far more powerful than American unions and extremely vociferous when it comes to the defense of entitlements. Thus, when the French government tried to bring a small measure of fiscal rectitude to that country's social security scheme in 1995, Paris was brought to a standstill with strikes and demonstrations.

At a recent conference in Italy, I heard Italian policy makers warn of an extremely bleak outlook based on zero (and perhaps negative) population growth, a "pension deficit" that already accounts for half the country's massive budget deficit and is growing worse by the day, and a public mentality accustomed and acculturated to extraordinary government generosity.

And Italy is not alone. These problems pervade European governments.

The issue of who's situation is worse—Europe's or America's—is obviously a pointless debate. The real point is that all over the industrial world, the demographics and political economy of aging are becoming Public Policy Issue Number

---

* A 1996 World Bank study *Global Capital Supply and Demand: Is There Enough to Go Around* documents the "unsustainability of current Social Security policies." It reports that the present value of unfunded pension liabilities in major European countries ranges from 150 to 250 percent of GDP. "This means that the implicit social security debt is a multiple of an already large explicit public debt which . . . averages more than 70 percent of GDP in industrial countries, up from 40 percent just fifteen years ago."

One. This set of issues is on its way to becoming the transcendent domestic agenda throughout the developed world.

Japan's case is somewhat different. Although the aging society is a major issue in Japan, too (indeed, owing to Japan's unique demography the age wave hits in full force there much sooner than elsewhere), the Japanese are somewhat better equipped to handle the challenge. Their savings rates are not just high, but the highest in the developed world. And while one should not minimize the problem of creeping entitlement spending in Japan, they have never quite embraced the European or American lust for entitling everyone without regard to funding.

Most important, unlike Americans, the Japanese are unencumbered by the illusion that their people are entitled to live the last third of their adult lives in subsidized leisure: What government gives can also be taken back if such savings are deemed to be in the public's long-term interest. In 1986, when Japan enacted a major reduction in pension benefits, the Ministry of Health and Welfare issued a concise justification that cited "equity between the generations." Few if any objections were heard in a society where most of the elderly at all income levels live with their extended families. In a statement issued the day he assumed office, Japan's new Prime Minister, Ryutaro Hashimoto, referred to the "imminent arrival of our Aging Society" as a priority imperative. Citing much greater life expectancy and a much reduced fertility rate, he went on to tell the Diet that Japan would have to "overhaul those social arrangements premised upon a life span of two score and ten to suit our new expected life span of fourscore."[5] Do we recall any American President ever making such a statement at *any* point in his term, let alone in the equivalent of an inaugural address?

Outside Europe, many developing countries are beginning to follow Japan's "Asian" model. Even many developing

countries, with populations still much younger than our own, are preparing for their demographic future with astonishing resolution. In South Korea, where the household savings rate runs at about 35 percent, companies routinely flaunt such shop-floor banners as WORKING TO MAKE A BETTER LIFE FOR THE NEXT GENERATION. In Singapore, workers' account balances in the Central Provident Fund—Singapore's mandatory pension savings system—now total nearly three quarters of GDP. In Chile, the average worker owns $21,000 worth of assets in the fifteen-year-old national funded retirement system—a sum about four times the average annual Chilean wage. Argentina, Peru, and Colombia are following Chile's lead and setting up funded systems of their own. Here, nothing has been saved in any national retirement system for workers to own.

3

Unsustainable Promises

The economist—and sometimes humorist—Herbert Stein likes to say, "If something is unsustainable, it tends to stop." Or as the old adage advises, "If your horse dies, we suggest you dismount."

We cannot finance the unfinanceable. By the year 2013, as Baby Boomers retire en masse, the annual surplus of Social Security tax revenues over outlays will disappear and turn negative. By 2030, when all the Boomers will have reached sixty-five, Social Security will be running an *annual* cash deficit of $766 billion. If Medicare Hospital Insurance is included and if both programs continue according to current law, the combined cash deficit that year will be $1.7 trillion. The horse, in other words, will be quite dead. By 2040, the deficit will probably hit $3.2 trillion; by 2050, $5.7 trillion.[1] Even discounting inflation, by 2050 the deficit for these two senior programs alone will come to approximately $700 *billion—over four times* the size of the *entire* federal deficit in 1996. Long before then, we will have had no choice but to dismount.

Social Security now has a small annual cash surplus but will begin to run large annual cash deficits around 2015.

Annual operating balance of the Social Security (Old-Age, Survivors, and Disability Insurance) trust funds: official "intermediate" projection

1995
$29
billion

2020   2025   2030   2035   2040

−$232
billion

−$482
billion

−$766
billion

−$1,051
billion

−$1,321
billion

SOURCE: Social Security Administration (1995)

Medicare *already* runs annual cash deficits that are projected to grow explosively in the next century.

Annual operating balance of the Medicare (Hospital Insurance) trust fund: official "intermediate" projection

1995   2010   2020   2030   2040

−$9
billion

−$116
billion

−$352
billion

−$934
billion

−$1,923
billion

SOURCE: Social Security Administration (1995)

Wall Street has yet to react to these obviously unfinanceable numbers. But it will. Since financial markets try to anticipate future events, the reaction will surely come years before the first Boomers start retiring on Social Security in 2008, when and if the markets determine that America has irretrievably lost any chance to deal with this challenge in advance. Should this occur, we will almost certainly see a fullscale economic emergency as interest rates roar into outer space.

Apologists for the status quo dismiss these numbers as "mere projections." So let me emphasize that the Social Security and Medicare projections I have cited are *official* projections, calculated by federal actuaries and economists working for the Social Security and Health Care Financing Administrations. These same experts also calculate an alternative, and much worse, high-cost projection. Historically, the high-cost projection has proved more accurate than the forecast I have used here. Moreover, the retirement and medical-care needs of the Boomer generation are by no means hypothetical. The Social Security Administration's former chief actuary A. Haeworth Robertson recently pointed out to me that 96 percent of senior benefits payable over the next seventy-five years will go to people who are already alive (and therefore countable) today.

Well, say the skeptics, if we can't borrow trillions of dollars, maybe we can raise taxes a bit and muddle through. But this isn't a viable option either. Let's start with the political fact that both parties in Washington are currently promoting a tax *cut,* though they debate its size. A tax hike is unmentionable. Then, consider the magnitude of the tax hikes we would need. By 2040, the cost of Social Security as a share of workers' payroll is projected to rise from today's 11.5 percent to 17 or 22 percent—depending on whether you accept SSA's "intermediate" or "high-cost" projection. Add to this both parts of Medicare, which currently cost the equivalent of 5.3

percent of payroll but are growing so rapidly that they will eventually overtake and surpass Social Security in size, and we're talking about 35 to 55 percent of every worker's paycheck before we even start to pay for the rest of what government does.[2]

It has always struck me as more than a bit disingenuous that defenders of the status quo on Social Security often pronounce in favor of big tax cuts for the "overtaxed middle class." Yet, by refusing to support reform now, they are opening the door to what could be the largest middle class tax hikes imaginable in order to keep the system solvent.

Obviously, such huge tax hikes could destroy the economy, to say nothing of the taxpayers*—which raises the interesting question of whether American workers can be expected to comply with them. The experience of runaway pension systems in Latin America and Eastern Europe suggests that if payroll taxes begin even to approach these levels, tax evasion will become widespread, and much of the economy will move into the tax-exempt "gray market." In other words, it may be impossible to fund the future cost of our current benefit promises no matter how willing we are to legislate higher tax rates.

This is doubly true if you consider that Social Security and Medicare are only part of the problem. We will also have to pay for Medicaid, whose budget for nursing home care will swell under the impact of the burgeoning number of old old. And we will have to pay for federal pensions, for veterans' benefits, for Supplemental Security Income (SSI), and for many other smaller public benefit programs. Today, total government benefit outlays (including state and local spend-

---

* It is important to realize that nearly half of workers now pay more in payroll taxes than in income taxes. If we include both the employee and employer FICA, the share is about four-fifths. Among young workers, close to nine in ten pay more in total FICA taxes. See *1994 Green Book* (House Ways and Means Committee, 1994).

By 2040, the cost of Social Security alone is projected to rise from 11% to between 17% and 22% of workers' payroll.

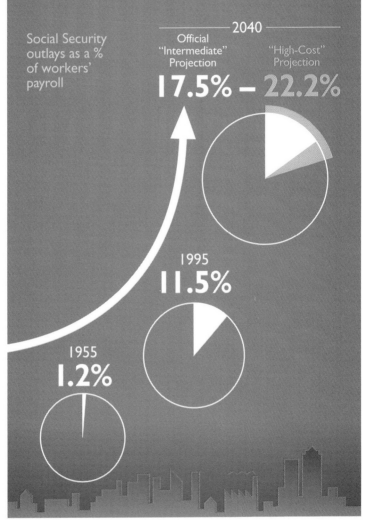

Social Security outlays as a % of workers' payroll

2040

Official "Intermediate" Projection

"High-Cost" Projection

17.5% – 22.2%

1995
11.5%

1955
1.2%

SOURCE: Social Security Administration (1995)

By 2040, the cost of Social Security and Medicare is projected to rise from 17% to between 35% and 55% of workers' payroll.

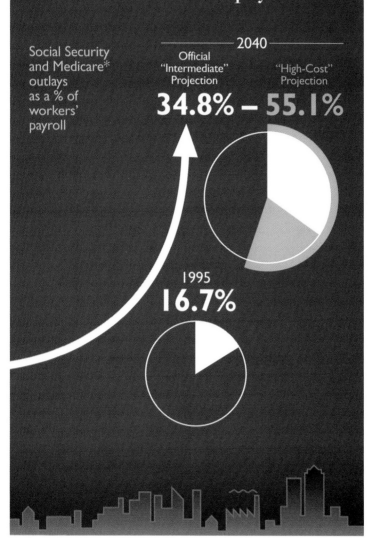

Social Security and Medicare* outlays as a % of workers' payroll

—————— 2040 ——————

Official "Intermediate" Projection

"High-Cost" Projection

34.8% – 55.1%

1995

16.7%

SOURCE: Social Security Administration (1995)
*Medicare includes both Hospital Insurance and Supplementary Medical Insurance.

ing) consume about 14 percent of GDP. According to projections based on SSA's intermediate scenario, total benefit outlays will hit 23.5 percent of GDP by the year 2040.[3] That's the equivalent of about two-thirds of every worker's taxable payroll.

Moreover, SSA's official scenario is probably too optimistic—particularly in its assumptions about future longevity and real wage growth. To be prudent, we should use the high-cost scenario, which depends on demographic and economic assumptions that better reflect our historical experience over the past few decades. According to that scenario, total benefits by the year 2040 will rise to 34.1 percent of GDP—or the equivalent of about nine-tenths of every worker's taxable payroll.

What would be the impact on future living standards if these scenarios actually came to pass? The first scenario would eliminate *all* real gains in after-tax wages from now to the year 2040 while the second scenario would cause a catastrophic decline of 59 percent. Neither scenario assumes any new program or benefit. Neither allows for economic emergencies, political crises, or foreign-policy threats over the next half century like those that have occurred during any other fifty years in the history of our nation. And incredibly, neither (not even the more pessimistic scenario) assumes that real health-care costs will continue to rise at historical rates. Yet either scenario (even the more optimistic) would spell the end of the American Dream.

Without fundamental entitlement reform, there is no escape from these dismal scenarios—not even the dangerous route of deliberate inflation. Social Security and federal pensions, after all, are fully indexed for inflation—as, in effect, are benefits under Medicare and Medicaid. Yes, revving up the printing presses at Treasury could reduce the cost of servicing the publicly held national debt, which is fixed in nominal dollars. But as anyone familiar with the history of twentieth-century Ger-

many can attest, the economic and social consequences of run-away inflation can be even more catastrophic than the consequences of runaway payroll taxes.

When I raise the long-term projections with defenders of the entitlements status quo, I find they don't directly dispute them. Instead, they look for ways to make the entire issue undiscussable. One is to insist that we talk about each program singly so that we can say: Well, Social Security retirement benefits alone won't kill tomorrow's taxpayers, nor will Disability Insurance, nor will Medicare Hospital Insurance, nor will civil service pensions, nor will military pensions, and so on. It's like saying no single snowflake matters in the avalanche that buries you. Another tactic is to say that there exists some magic solution ("comprehensive health-care reform," for instance) that entirely solves the problem but which for political reasons is blocked, and so therefore we shouldn't discuss any part of the problem. Still another tactic, and the most perverse, is to say, Why worry about projections that are so patently unsustainable that they obviously won't be allowed to happen? The reason, of course, is so that we can plan for gradual and humane reforms now—rather than enact brutal cuts later, in the midst of economic and social crisis.

Thus far, America's reaction to the disaster that looms ahead offers a new answer to the old question about what happens when an irresistible force meets an immovable object: We close our eyes. Or else we invent comforting myths to hide the unpleasant facts.

Consider two images. The preferred assumption in Washington is that a growing underclass has triggered a massive explosion in welfare spending—shattering the federal budget and impoverishing taxpayers. Meanwhile, to the extent that our political leaders discuss Social Security, they usually depict a stable vessel—the S.S. *Trust Fund*—floating serenely into the next century. The icebergs are so far over the horizon as to be of no real concern.

Keeping these images in mind, let us compare a few numbers. From 1970 to 1995, a period that covers most of the historical welfare explosion, the number of recipients of Aid to Families with Dependent Children (AFDC), our principal cash welfare benefit, grew by seven million. At today's average annual federal cost of $877 per person, this "explosion" added about $6 billion to total annual federal outlays.

Now let's turn to the next twenty-five years. From 1995 to 2020, the number of Social Security beneficiaries is projected to rise by twenty-five million. At an average annual federal cost of $9,309 per person by 2020 (in 1995 dollars), this trend will add $232 billion to total annual federal outlays.[4] If, as many claim, the history of AFDC is "catastrophic," does a word exist to describe the future of Social Security? It is true that concerns about welfare arise not simply from its cost but from the social pathology it institutionalizes. But why do we ignore the perverse incentives in Social Security that discourage families from saving and preparing for the future, incentives that could do far greater harm to our economy and society than welfare dependency?

Despite the inevitable consequences, the senior lobby asserts that American workers are duty bound to fulfill their side of an ill-defined "contract between generations." Yet one group's "earned right" to a benefit is another group's "unearned obligation" to pay a tax, and it is this second group to which our children and grandchildren belong. Understandably, they are suspicious of a binding contract to which they never agreed—so suspicious that younger Americans are more likely to believe in UFOs than that they'll ever receive a dime in Social Security benefits.

There's an old adage about robbing Peter to pay Paul. In this entitlement shell game, we're proposing to rob Peter Jr. to pay Peter Sr.—even when the Peter Sr. in question may not need the money. In fact, Peter Jr. is already paying plenty. Because so much of Social Security is tax free and because re-

More young people believe in UFOs than think they will ever receive Social Security.

% of poll respondents age 18–34 who think…

…UFOs exist now

46%

…Social Security will exist by the time they retire

28%

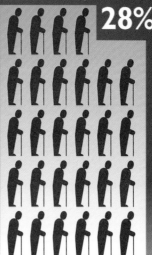

SOURCE: Third Millennium (1994)

tirees no longer pay FICA taxes, a typical retired couple on Social Security in 1994 with $30,000 in total cash income paid, on average, only $790 in total federal taxes. Meanwhile, their son and daughter-in-law, struggling to raise a child on the same income, paid $7,035 in total federal taxes (including both the employer and the employee FICA tax), nearly nine times as much![5] No other industrial nation tilts its tax burden away from the elderly—or its benefits system toward them—as unfairly as the United States does.

Defenders of the current system misleadingly describe Social Security and Medicare as "insurance" or "pension" programs and claim that beneficiaries are only getting back what they paid in. They're wrong. The vast majority of today's beneficiaries are getting back *far more* than they and their employers ever paid in via FICA contributions (even including interest). Given an average life expectancy, the typical one-earner couple retiring in 1995 will get about $123,000 more from Social Security than the average earner and his or her employers *ever* paid into it, plus interest. Omit the employer's contribution and calculate only the payback on the personal taxes paid by the employee, and the windfall rises to $173,000. With Medicare thrown in, it rises to nearly $310,000, much of it tax free. These are not earned benefits but unearned windfalls—which is why I have long favored requiring the Social Security Administration to issue regular reports to retirees showing how much they have received and how much they have contributed. Moreover, these are windfalls which our children and grandchildren will have to pay for and which they will never enjoy themselves. If you're a typical single male who retired in 1980, you're getting a Social Security windfall of $39,000 above and beyond your FICA contributions and your employer's, plus interest. But a typical single male retiring in 2010 will suffer a net loss of $36,000; for a high-earning single male, the net loss will be $135,000.[6]

A typical couple retiring today will receive far more in Social Security and Medicare benefits than the value of their prior contributions plus interest.

Payback* in excess of Social Security and Medicare† contributions plus interest, in constant 1993 dollars

Social Security and Medicare payback on employee contributions only

+$308,000

Social Security payback on employee contributions only

+$173,000

Social Security payback on employee and employer contributions

+$123,000

SOURCE: Eugene Steuerle, *Retooling Social Security for the 21st Century* (1994)
*Paybacks are for a one-earner couple with average wage history retiring at age 65 in 1995.
†Social Security is Old-Age and Survivors Insurance only; Medicare includes both Hospital Insurance and Supplementary Medical Insurance.

In any case, since FICA contributions have never been saved by the federal government, the point is moot: Regardless of what you paid in, the Social Security "trust fund" now holds, on your behalf, nothing but claims on future taxpayers. The term "trust fund" may suggest a vault in which everyone's Social Security taxes are stacked up to be paid out later. But the Social Security trust fund is the ultimate fiscal oxymoron. The "assets," which are supposed to keep the system solvent until the year 2030, are simply Treasury IOUs. When it comes time to redeem these claims and the interest they will have accumulated, the Treasury will have to raise the cash by borrowing from the public or by taxing the public. Either way, absent any policy change, future taxpayers will have to pay again for today's much-vaunted Social Security "surpluses." It might be more honest to call it a "distrust fund."

If the Social Security and Medicare balance sheets were evaluated according to private-sector accounting standards, both would be declared massively insolvent immediately. Consider that the federal government has already promised to today's adults $8 trillion in future Social Security benefits beyond the value of the taxes they have paid to date—a figure more than 250 times greater than the much decried "unfunded liabilities" of *all* private-sector pension plans in America! If Congress were required by law to fund Social Security the way private pensions must be funded, the annual federal deficit would instantly rise by some $650 billion. Add in our lavish federal employee pensions, which are also unfunded, and the deficit would rise by about $765 billion. Add in Medicare, and today's deficit would rise by nearly $1.4 trillion.[7] Private-sector executives who ran their pension systems this way would be thrown in jail for wholesale violation of federal regulations.

Defenders of the current system claim that these unfunded liabilities don't matter because government, unlike a private employer, can't go out of business and hence will never have

The unfunded liabilities for Social Security and federal pensions alone total $9.5 trillion—or about 300 times the combined unfunded liabilities of *all* private pension plans in the United States.

Unfunded benefit liabilities, in present-value dollars, at end of FY 1995 (federal) and at end of 1994 (private)

Total: $9.5 trillion

Social Security: $8.0 trillion

Federal pensions: $1.5 trillion

Total: $31 billion

Private pension system

Federal retirement programs

SOURCE: Office of Management and Budget (1996); Social Security Administration (1996); Pension Benefit Guaranty Corporation (1995); and author's calculations

If the federal government accounted for its retirement liabilities the way private companies must account for their pension liabilities, the official annual federal deficit would rise by nearly $800 billion.

Federal deficit with and without amortization charge for unfunded benefit liabilities*

Total:
$930 billion

Social Security:
$650 billion

Federal pensions:
$120 billion

Official deficit:
$160 billion

Total:
$160 billion

Official deficit in FY 1995

Deficit in FY 1995 with honest accounting for federal retirement programs

SOURCE: Office of Management and Budget (1996); Social Security Administration (1996); Congressional Budget Office (1995); and author's calculations
*Liabilities are amortized over 30 years on an ERISA (Employee Retirement Income Security Act) basis.

to pay off its benefit obligations all at once. This misses the point. The significance of unfunded federal benefit liabilities has nothing to do with the risk of bankruptcy. These liabilities are a measure of the net gift we are asking from taxpayers in future years to cover benefit promises that have already accrued in past years and are important *precisely because the government is not expected to go out of business.* To the extent that these promises are deemed unbreakable, they will have to be paid off, just like the publicly held national debt. When confronted with this logic, apologists sometimes take another tack. The liabilities don't matter, they say, because government (again unlike a private employer) can always modify its benefit promises. The problem with this argument is not that it's untrue but that it's hypocritical. To the public at large, the defenders of the current system say that Social Security works "just like a pension," or is "money-back insurance," or is based on "an inviolable generational contract." To the critics who know better, they say, Don't worry; if it comes to that, we can always cut benefits.

Meanwhile, Congress has attempted to ban what the policy wonks call unfunded mandates—federal laws that impose costs on the states without providing funding. That's fine— but worrying about such mandates while ignoring Social Security and Medicare is like mistaking Woody Allen for Arnold Schwarzenegger. Social Security and Medicare are *the mother of all unfunded mandates.*

It's time to face up to the awful truth that trust-fund accounting is a hoax, that Social Security is a vast Ponzi scheme in which only the first people in are big winners and the vast array of those who join late in the game lose. Today's payroll taxes go directly from the pockets of today's workers straight to the mailboxes of today's retirees after a brief stop at the federal Treasury. Since FICA is a tax and tax revenues are fungible, any annual surplus of FICA taxes over benefits is "loaned" by Social Security to the Treasury, which uses the

money to pay for other government programs. A trust-fund ledger for such transfers is a waste of time. Does it really help to know that Social Security is a bit richer and Treasury is a bit poorer? Given the apparent congressional appetite for constitutional amendments, why not consider one banning government trust funds?

As Federal Reserve Chairman Alan Greenspan told the Kerrey-Danforth Entitlement Commission on which I recently served, the only bottom line that really counts is government's total borrowing balance with the public—otherwise known as the annual consolidated budget deficit or surplus. Transferring IOUs from the right pocket to the left pocket does nothing to bridge Social Security's and Medicare's future funding shortfall.

Along with this melancholy list of fiscal unsustainables, we should consider some sobering *moral unsustainables*. Social Security was established to protect the elderly from indigence—from "a poverty-ridden old age," to use FDR's phrase. If Social Security goes bankrupt subsidizing middle-class and affluent Americans, many of whom can live well enough without their benefits, what will happen to those who really do need Social Security? After all, Social Security accounts for more than half the total income of retirees making less than $20,000 a year, and these lower-income beneficiaries (about 15 million households in 1990) comprise about half of all Social Security recipients.[8] This sobering dependence demands deliberate and prudent foresight. Yet many political leaders imply by their inaction that it's fine to wait until trillion-dollar deficits have devastated the economy before slashing benefits at the last minute, when Americans at all income levels will have lost any chance at all to plan for their future. Millions of lower-income beneficiaries would then be stranded in what might be called a demographic depression as the safety net that Social Security was enacted to provide vanishes. With irony, future historians may someday

record that those who claimed to be Social Security's defenders were the very ones who most wanted to exempt the program from gradual and timely reform.

At a recent conference of The Concord Coalition, Warren Rudman suggested that we should judge our collective treatment of posterity by the same standards we judge our individual actions as heads of families. He regularly asks audiences to imagine a system of family finances that held children liable for their parents' personal debts. Every parent in the audience responds that this is unthinkable. Yet in effect, this is what we are doing collectively by passing on a $3.6-trillion public debt and a $17-trillion mountain of unfunded benefit liabilities. Who do we suppose is going to pay these bills?

Paul Tsongas likes to say, "It's not enough for our children to love us. We should want them to respect us." Over a century and a half ago, Alexis de Tocqueville wrote prophetically in *Democracy in America* that "[t]he American republic will endure until the politicians find they can bribe the people with their own money." It's worse than that: It's our children's money. When our children look into the Social Security trust fund and find nothing there but IOUs with themselves named as *payers*, they will surely wonder how we could have treated them so shabbily.

4

The Inescapable Bottom Line

I often reflect on the stunning transformations I have witnessed in America since my generation came of age after World War II. Youth, back then, was not just a personal but a collective frame of mind. We had just triumphed over global depression and fascism, and our eyes were fixed on a bright future for which we had all sacrificed, planned, and saved.

It was an era when economists measured growth by a society's ability to amass capital, and middle-class families eagerly embraced new ways—pension plans, savings accounts, and insurance policies—to accumulate household savings. It was an era when big government was regarded by both friends and enemies as an engine of investment—running surpluses, investing billions in world peace, and feverishly building highways, harbors, research laboratories, and universities. Most of all, it was an era when voters willingly footed the tax bill for endowments that would outlive them. Hard-nosed yet soft-hearted elders, who had never seen a government check, were proud to watch grandchildren still in

their twenties race past them economically. In those years, production boomed while living standards and birth rates soared.

In retrospect, demographers and economists call mine the fortunate generation, a description that would have mystified me in my youth but now seems obvious. Born the lucky child of working-class immigrants, I have since become the affluent yet anxious parent of young adults whose generation has been cut adrift as America abandons its fundamental commitment to our national future. This loss, perhaps triggered by hubris after our massive wartime and post-war success, has had fateful repercussions. By the end of the 1980s, a bipartisan embrace of borrow-and-spend fiscal policy had reduced our savings rate to the vanishing point and piled up a mountain of IOUs to foreign creditors unprecedented in world history. In the last fifteen years, the ratio of federal debt to GDP—what many economists consider the most crucial indicator of fiscal probity—has doubled.

Somewhere along the way, most of the buoyant language with which we once celebrated the American Dream vanished. "Upward mobility" gave way to "wage stagnation," "lifting all boats" turned into a "zero-sum game," "melting pot" became "multiculturalism," "growth dividend" is now "debt overhang." Once, we assumed that when our children grew up they'd have a better life than ours. Now, we have every reason to fear the generational wrath of those who'll do worse.

Not long ago, Congress debated how best to assure our children's future—how to build smarter schools, safer suburbs, a stronger defense. Today, we argue over how best to provide a comfortable retirement for our elders—how to make marginal adjustments in a trillion-dollar flood of retirement and health benefits promoted by dozens of powerful lobbies, flowing to all Americans over age sixty-five regardless of need.

During the post-war American high, we paid off huge wartime debts. Since 1980, however, the national debt has exploded again.

Gross and net federal debt as a % of GDP at end of fiscal year*

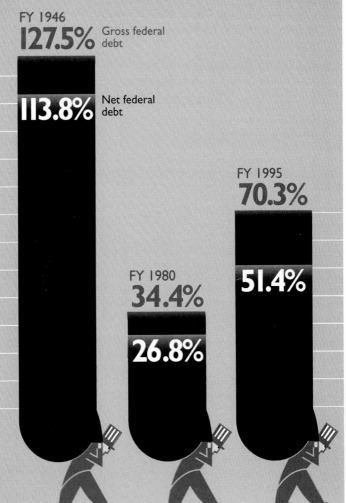

FY 1946
127.5% Gross federal debt

113.8% Net federal debt

FY 1995
70.3%

FY 1980
34.4%

51.4%

26.8%

SOURCE: Council of Economic Advisers (1996)
*Net debt is debt held by the public; gross debt is debt held by the public plus intragovernmental debt held by federal trust funds.

The late 1990s will probably be dominated by anxiety about our future. Polls show that most of us now feel that we have abandoned our fundamentals and become fearful about the prospects for our children. Headlines proclaim "sullen" voters, "downsizing" employers, "revolutionary" agendas, "train wreck" budget struggles, and "realigned" electorates. A consensus is gathering that the American Dream is in jeopardy, yet we have not begun to appreciate the magnitude of our challenge or the difficulty of regaining some measure of what we have lost. Most Americans still hope that our problems will be solved by this year's budget deal or next year's Dow Jones high or—perhaps by the year 2000—the economic payoff of an emerging information highway.

It's time to wake up: These fixes, even if they work out, are not even a serious first step.

Notwithstanding its strengths, many real and some imagined, the American economy since the early 1970s has failed at what matters most: *raising productivity*. Why should the average American care about such a seemingly abstract concept? Because working longer hours to produce more goods and services—or putting everyone's spouse (or child) to work—is not the way to raise living standards. A higher standard of living means producing more while working the same or fewer hours—in other words, being more productive. Only rising productivity will lift real (after inflation) hourly compensation and take-home pay. The astute economist Paul Krugman sums it up this way: "Productivity isn't everything, but in the long run it is almost everything. A country's ability to improve its standard of living over time depends almost entirely on its ability to raise its output per worker."[1] If Krugman is right—and he is—Americans have good reason for concern.

Since the early 1970s, real U.S. national income per full-time worker (as calculated by the Commerce Department) has grown by approximately 0.4 percent per year. Total

worker compensation has grown at about the same meager pace, a rate of growth so low that a debate rages among economists over whether—after accounting for inflation and the rising costs of employer-paid health care—the typical U.S. worker has enjoyed any perceptible wage growth at all since 1973, way back when Richard Nixon was in the White House. Meanwhile, in Japan and the European Community, real output per worker over the same time period has grown by 50 to 70 percent, and average real wages have risen by 40 to 50 percent.[2] Unemployment has been higher in Europe than in the United States, it is true. But we, in turn, are leading the developed world in the growth of an unemployable underclass.

Along with the aging of America itself, which we can do little or nothing to slow, low productivity is the primary reason the fiscal projections are so bleak. Unless we raise productivity substantially, we will not be able to afford even sharply reduced benefits to tomorrow's retirees without impoverishing tomorrow's workers. And so whenever productivity recovers during the early phases of an economic expansion, we celebrate. And whenever it falls again as the expansion slows, leaving the long-term trend unchanged, we await a miraculous intercession.

Some put their faith in deregulation and lower marginal tax rates. Though the reasons for our poor productivity performance are complex and hotly debated, most economists agree that stricter regulation played at least some role in the initial 1970s slowdown—and that relieving industry of capricious federal mandates would help the economy today. And few deny that lowering tax rates might do *something* to encourage innovation and more work effort—and hence boost economic output. But enthusiasts for deregulation and tax cuts seldom ask why our major European competitors, though they are burdened by far *higher* taxes and *more* regu-

lation than we are,* have nonetheless achieved rates of productivity and real wage growth averaging several times our own.

Others subscribe to a high-tech gospel which teaches that innovations in information and communications technologies are about to transform the workplace in ways that will push productivity to breathtaking new heights. No one doubts that technological innovation is fundamental to productivity growth. But to exploit these new technologies, we will need a surge of new investment—which in turn requires greatly increased savings. We thus arrive at the inescapable bottom line insisted on by economists from Adam Smith to Karl Marx to Alfred Marshall to John Maynard Keynes to Paul Samuelson: No country can enjoy sustained productivity growth without investing, and no country can sustain high investment for long without saving.

These economists understood that productivity depends on many underlying conditions—from the pace of technological innovation to efficient and fluid markets and an industrious and educated workforce. But they all agreed that capital formation is a *necessary* condition for productivity growth. Economists use the term "capital formation" to describe both savings and investment. It includes not just warehouses and smokestacks but (at least in theory) any resource we dedicate to enriching our future. Spending on public infrastructure, research and development, education, and worker training are all examples of capital formation. Looked at another way, capital formation is the aggregate measure of everything that society, either privately or publicly, *refrains from consuming today for the sake of a higher payoff tomorrow.* According to

---

* Besides being burdened by higher taxes and more regulation (or perhaps because of it), Europeans are also less entrepreneurial than Americans. As a leading European business friend of mine recently said, "Europe is good at producing capital but not capitalists."

some economists, the rate at which a country accumulates capital may account for as much as two thirds of its rate of growth in real output per worker.

Let me repeat: Capital formation means consuming less today in order to realize a higher payoff tomorrow. From some on the right, we still hear the old supply-side refrain: Just cut taxes, and economic growth will soar. From some on the left, we hear that lower interest rates will spur the economy to new heights.* But with productivity, as with everything else, there's no such thing as a free lunch. Long-term growth can only be achieved the old-fashioned way: We will have to earn it by saving and investing more.

Capital formation is not only crucial to productivity growth; it is also the one determinant of productivity growth which a society can directly control. We cannot legislate new technological breakthroughs—such as the invention of room-temperature fusion—but we can legislate a balanced budget. When the federal government runs a budget deficit, it subtracts dollar for dollar from the pool of private savings available for private business investment; when government reduces its deficit, it adds dollar for dollar to that pool. It may not matter to private savers whether their dollars end up building a machine, training a worker, or purchasing a Treasury bond. But it matters a great deal to the economy. Investment in new machines and trained workers is likely to raise the economy's productivity and income. A Treasury bond will not. Government can also increase our pool of in-

---

* My own view of the role of monetary policy is that recently expressed by William McDonough, President of the New York Federal Reserve Bank, in a speech before the Annual Financial Services Forum of the New York State Bankers Association: "[W]hat monetary policy cannot do, in and of itself, is produce economic growth. Economic growth stems from increases in the supply of capital and labor and from the productivity with which labor and capital are used, neither of which is directly influenced by monetary policy. However, without doubt, monetary policy can help foster economic growth by ensuring a stable price environment."

vestible savings by changing tax policies so that they reward the savings efforts of business and households—for example, by taxing consumption. Finally, the government can contribute to capital formation itself by making collective investments in public goods—such as rapid transit or better schools—that create future returns for the whole economy.

Of course, nothing is as simple as it sounds. For one thing, the relationship between higher savings and investment on the one hand and higher productivity and income growth on the other is necessarily a long-term affair. Its decisive impact shows up not over two or three years but over two or three decades. For another, it's not the only thing that matters. Sometimes productivity surges forward (the transistor is invented) or falls back (oil prices jump) for reasons that have little to do with capital formation in prior years. Sometimes societies think they're engaging in productivity-enhancing capital formation when they're not. The Soviet Union spent prodigious sums on dams and steel mills that actually hurt living standards because the resources were "invested" by central planners who placed little importance on the actual economic returns. *Quality of investment thus matters as much as quantity.* On this score, there is some evidence that our less regulated, more entrepreneurial, more open and fluid economy makes it possible for American companies to get a bigger productivity bang per investment buck than others in the more regulated and closed economies. However, when others are saving so much more than we are, their sheer quantity can overwhelm our superior quality. And sometimes, even when we're making productivity-enhancing investments, there's still no reliable way of calculating the benefit. Few would deny that raising honest and drug-free kids constitutes a genuine benefit to our national future. But few would ever dare quantify it in economic terms.

Still, even if we allow for these caveats (and even if we just look at physical investment, which is all we know how to

measure), history has repeatedly borne out what the great economic thinkers tell us: There is a strong link between capital formation and productivity. Indeed, I know of no major economy, yesterday or today, that has ever sustained high rates of productivity growth without high rates of savings and investment. Since the 1950s, productivity growth in each of the major industrial market economies has been very closely correlated with its rate of investment. Situated at the extreme high end of the investment "input" and productivity "output" distribution is Japan. At the extreme low end—you guessed it—is the United States.

By emphasizing savings and investment, I am appealing to a tradition long rooted in our past, a tradition that has contributed to the prosperity of my generation and to that of the generations before it. But in recent decades, "thrift" has acquired negative connotations of pointless and even painful austerity. Or it evokes pictures of pinched and parsimonious country clubbers thinking of their own future and no one else's. But the word "thrift" stems from the verb "to thrive"—which, in turn, means to prosper and flourish. When our nation was founded, Ben Franklin celebrated the word "thrift" to describe individuals who succeed by dint of dedicated attention to their future. At about the same time, Adam Smith used the word to describe entire societies that do the same. Connecting the personal to the collective—and the economic to the ethical—this word probably defines the nature of our challenge better than any other.

But thrift is precisely what we've forgotten. From an average of 8.1 percent of GDP in the 1960s, the U.S. net national savings rate dipped to 7.2 percent in the 1970s, then plunged to 3.9 percent in the 1980s and to 2.3 percent thus far in the 1990s. While public dissaving (that is, federal deficits) has recently pushed net national savings to near zero, private savings have plunged as well—from well over 8 percent of GDP in the 1960s and 1970s to barely 5 percent in the 1990s. U.S.

net domestic investment has fallen in tandem, from 7.3 percent of GDP in the 1960s to 3.5 percent in the 1990s—a decline that would have been much steeper if we had not turned from investing abroad to borrowing abroad.[3] This economic change reflects a huge change in American behavior.

Some critics will say that I've got things backwards—and that the decline in U.S. rates of savings and investment since the 1960s is the consequence, not the cause, of slower growth in productivity and living standards. In this view, Americans are saving less because the slowdown in real wage growth has left them with less income to save. As with most economic theories, there is an ounce of truth in this one—but only an ounce. The reality is that there is a negative feedback between flagging rates of savings and investment and slowly growing incomes. Lower rates of capital formation lead to lower productivity and income growth. Faced with slower than expected growth in incomes, people react by saving less in order (over the short term) to maintain the living standard they have become accustomed to. But by saving less, they cause productivity and income growth to slow still more in a vicious downward spiral.

Other critics say that the real problem is not a lack of savings but a lack of investment opportunities. It's obviously true that incentives to invest are just as important as incentives to save and that if returns on new investments are poor (or negative), there will be less new investment. But savings and investment are different sides of the same equation. In a market economy like ours, interest rates go up or down to ensure that the demand for one matches the supply of the other. I find it hard to believe that if U.S. savings rates were adequate to meet investment demand, real interest rates would be stuck at historically high levels and we would still be importing great quantities of foreign capital. The real issue is not whether we have a "shortage" of savings or of investment opportunities but how much a given increment to capital for-

mation will increase productivity and national income—and whether we are willing to forgo some more consumption today in order to enjoy a higher living standard tomorrow.

Still other critics will say, Just hang on a minute, Pete Peterson. What's this obsession with *savings rates*? You of all people should know that what matters is *net worth*—and that because of the current boom in the stock market, Americans and America are in fact quickly growing wealthier. What possible difference to the economy does it make if that extra wealth comes from the appreciation of assets rather than from a higher savings rate?

The answer is that it can make a great deal of difference indeed. Yes, a higher stock market means that Americans are wealthier—at least to the extent that the increase in average net financial worth has not been offset by losses in other types of investments. Remember: Inflated commercial real estate took a beating in the late eighties and inflated residential real estate took a beating in the early nineties. However, a higher stock market does not necessarily mean that the productive capacity of our economy has increased any more than higher real estate prices reflect an actual increase in the size or beauty of our houses. When the stock market rises, U.S. plant and equipment for the moment are worth that much more. (I say for the moment because the extraordinary stock market boom since 1982 should not be counted on to last forever.) But has this released *new* real resources from consumption uses to investment uses? The answer is no. What determines the economy's productive capacity is the net annual addition to the nation's real capital stock—not the change in the market value of assets. Historically, changes in stock prices have not even been a particularly good indirect predictor of future productivity, for stock prices reflect many factors. The market can rise because capital is suddenly deemed to be scarcer, or because investors expect a change in interest rates or in capital gains rates, or for a dozen other reasons that have no

necessary relation to future productivity. This is why the official measures of *economic* savings—from the Commerce Department's National Income and Product Accounts to the Federal Reserve Board's Flow of Funds Accounts—all define savings as the share of current income we refrain from consuming and instead dedicate to new investments.

Some of my critics concede that I am right about the importance of current savings for economic growth, but wonder whether asset prices aren't more relevant in measuring the magnitude of our retirement challenge. Money in the bank, after all, is money in the bank. Can't a higher market bail the Boomers out?

Again, not necessarily. What we must consider is the aggregate behavior of all individual investors—and not all investors can cash in at the same price. Say the Dow Jones soars 1,000 percent by the time the Boomers retire. Perhaps Joe Boomer can sell his stock and move to Jackson Hole. But can seventy-six million Boomers? Whatever means tomorrow's retirees use to exercise claims on tomorrow's production—whether Social Security transfers or private pension payouts or personal savings—those claims must come at the expense of workers' living standards *unless* they are accompanied by commensurate growth in GDP. Think about it: When the day arrives that Boomers (or their pension plans) start selling off assets en masse to pay for their retirement, *who will be the buyers?* If no one else is saving and if real interest rates are rising, the market value—dubbed the Great Depreciation by Craig Karpel in *The Retirement Myth*—of all assets will plunge proportionately. That plunge could be as much as 45 percent, according to economists John Shoven and Sylvester Schieber.[4] The truth is that capital income (as a component of GDP) cannot rise indefinitely faster than GDP. And what determines GDP growth is employment plus productivity—which leads us right back to the original issue: boosting savings and investment rates.

Nothing better illustrates the decline of our thrift ethic than the radical reversal in our view of deficit spending. If you look back at the history of the federal budget from George Washington through Dwight Eisenhower (and exclude only years of declared war and catastrophic depression), the fiscal record is remarkable: a mere 30 years of budget deficits versus 106 years of budget surpluses. Moreover, the deficits, on average, did not exceed 0.5 percent of the total economy. Since 1960, however, we have registered 35 years of deficits and only 1 year of surplus—and the deficits have averaged a far larger 2.7 percent of the total economy.

Until the 1960s, it was widely assumed by Americans that running a deficit to indulge our youthful impatience—at the expense of the flesh-and-blood youth of the next generation—was immoral and that whenever we were compelled to borrow publicly (during a war, for instance), we were duty bound to pay off the debt as soon as possible. Four years after the end of the Civil War, the secretary to the British legation in the United States noted, "The majority of Americans would appear disposed to endure any amount of sacrifice rather than bequeath a portion of their debt to future generations."[5] The same sentiment prevailed after both world wars. As recently as the late 1940s, we insisted on running large federal surpluses to pay back war debt even though a combat-weary public yearned for new consumer goods. And what modest outlays were made from the federal budget went largely for such investments as infrastructure and basic research.

Today, all that has changed. The uncontrolled growth in federal entitlements over the past three decades has given rise to a "structural deficit" economy. By borrowing to finance its deficits, the federal government drains our already shallow pool of private savings—and hence crowds out private investment. But private investment is not all that gets crowded

out. The headlong growth in entitlements has also squeezed public investment out of the federal budget itself. Of every nondefense dollar the federal government now spends, only about five cents go to build something tangible that remains standing after the fiscal year is over. In 1965, discretionary spending—the overall budget category that includes most general-interest, future-oriented spending—accounted for 69 percent of the federal budget. Today, it is 36 percent of the budget and dropping.[6]

Despite all the talk of revolution in Washington, the recent budget plans proposed by Congress and the White House constitute less a reversal than an acceleration of our current fiscal trajectory. The reason? They would slash general-interest spending in real dollars while only gently restraining the growth in entitlements. When I say slash, I'm not exaggerating. Under the fiscal year 1996 budget resolution passed by the House of Representatives, spending on space, science, and technology was slated for a real dollar cut of 27 percent between 1995 and 2002; spending on natural resources and the environment, for a cut of 31 percent; and spending on education and training, for a cut of 35 percent. Nor is it just the Republicans who would gut investment spending. Under the administration's final fiscal year 1996 proposal, floated just before budget negotiations collapsed in January, discretionary spending would, by 2002, actually be cut more deeply than under the GOP plan.[7] Democrats like to boast about reinvesting in America. But they will never find the dollars to do so if they stand by while senior benefits crowd out the rest of the budget.

Let's look at the numbers. Under Congress's fiscal year 1996 budget plan, senior benefits in 2002 would consume still another record share of federal spending—nearly 50 percent of noninterest outlays, up from 40 percent today and just 17 percent in 1965. Average benefits per senior would grow from $15,456 to about $17,300 in real inflation-

adjusted dollars. All other (noninterest) spending per capita would fall from $2,942 to about $2,500.[8] The year 2002 is still within a benign demographic period in which my relatively small generation (born before VJ Day) will be retiring and the relatively large Boomer generation (born after 1945) will be working and paying taxes. And remember: This is not the President's plan but the *Republican* plan, widely attacked as a "declaration of war" on America's seniors.

Recently, a General Accounting Office study concluded that we must invest $112 billion to bring the infrastructure of America's schools back to acceptable levels.[9] But where can we find such a sum when entitlements and interest on old debts crowd out everything else?* Since the 1950s, we have spent trillions on defense—much of it focused on neutralizing Soviet nuclear power. Today, we have a historic opportunity to de-nuclearize thousands of Soviet warheads at a time when their sale to rogue nations has become an unthinkable threat. Yet Congress finds it difficult to come up with the $3.5-billion pittance budgeted for this transcendentally important purpose. This perverse situation reminds Senator Sam Nunn of the Marx Brothers movie in which a gang of thieves enters with guns drawn while one of the Marx Brothers points a gun *at his own head* and says, "Stop or I'll shoot."

---

* Also crowded out by entitlements is any impulse to conduct major experiments that confront the amalgam of problems subsumed by the word "underclass." One study that particularly impressed me is the now classic 1985 Committee for Economic Development report *Investing in Our Children: Business and the Public Schools;* in it, a group of CEOs conclude unanimously that an additional $11 billion invested annually in the health, education, and skills of underclass kids would have an excellent economic and social payoff. This "Third World within our First World" defines the outer perimeters of our productivity, crime, and drug problems. Up to now, the problem of the underclass has proved to be intractable and is assumed to remain that way. This is not acceptable. We should be undertaking major initiatives now before this cancer metastasizes throughout our body politic. Yet we are most unlikely to do so under our current fiscally constrained circumstances. Indeed, can we imagine a politician today so brave as to suggest a major new social initiative and then say that we should meet the costs by raising taxes—in other words, by paying for it?

If we're already preparing to cannibalize everything from school lunches to space shuttles to stoke the senior entitlement furnace, what will we do when the age wave hits? Unless we change course, entitlements will consume *all* federal revenues by the mid-2020s.[10] Not a dime will be left over for national security—much less for vital domestic investment priorities.

To break out of our slow-growth, low-investment structural-deficit trap, we must control the exploding cost of senior benefits. But beyond that, to support our aging society, we must set an explicit productivity goal—then dedicate the physical and human resources to achieve it. A sensible objective is to increase the rate of growth in real per worker national income—in other words, productivity—by a full percentage point, from the post-1973 average of 0.4 percent to about 1.5 percent a year. Even this substantial increase will not equal American productivity growth rates in the 1950s and 1960s or match Japan's record during the 1970s and 1980s. But it would come close to returning U.S. productivity to its average rate of growth over the entire last century—and it would bring our growth close to that of most of our European competitors.

A one-percentage-point improvement in productivity growth may not seem like a lot.* But such differences, compounded over time, determine the fate of nations. Until recently, it was reasonable to assume that children would do better than their parents—and indeed, throughout most of

---

* Whether this improvement seems big or small depends on one's perspective. Consider: If each worker in the economy produces $10 in goods and services and productivity is growing at a 0.4 percent rate, the next year each worker will be producing $10.04; if productivity increases at a 1.5 percent rate, the next year each worker will be producing $10.15—or 1 percent more than at the 0.4 percent growth rate. On the other hand, if we focus on the percentage change in growth rates rather than the percentage change in output, even a relatively modest increase looks huge when the initial growth rate is tiny: 1.5 is 275 percent higher than 0.4.

On our current path, entitlements will eventually consume all federal revenue, leaving nothing to pay for interest on the national debt, much less defense, education, and other discretionary expenditures.

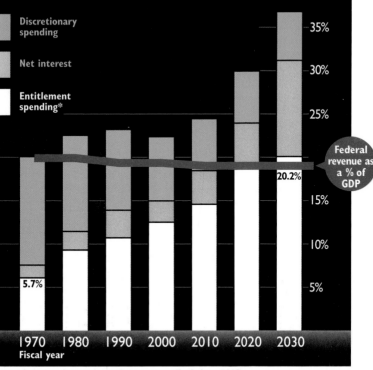

Federal outlays as a % of GDP

Discretionary spending

Net interest

Entitlement spending*

35%

30%

25%

Federal revenue as a % of GDP

20.2%

15%

10%

5.7%

5%

1970 1980 1990 2000 2010 2020 2030
Fiscal year

SOURCE: Bipartisan Commission on Entitlement and Tax Reform (1995)
*Entitlements are net of offsetting receipts such as Medicare premiums.

our history until the 1970s, U.S. living standards roughly doubled every generation, not just for the rich but for everyone. At our post-1973 rate of productivity growth, however, living standards will take 175 years to double.

Now consider what will happen if we meet my productivity goal: The time it takes for living standards to double will shrink to less than fifty years. By the time today's toddlers are ready to marry, inflation-adjusted private incomes will have grown by roughly 50 percent. So too will federal revenues (assuming today's tax rates). Not only will the senior boom be more affordable, so will everything else, from housing and health care to college educations and exotic vacations. As individuals and as citizens, we will have done better for ourselves and our children. We will have averted national decline and begun to restore the American Dream.

Recently, my fellow Nebraskan Warren Buffett shared with me his delightful (and insightful) tale of the Static Islanders, a small, isolated, and rapidly aging society. The descendants of castaways, these Static Islanders have forgotten the virtue of thrift—and the importance of productivity growth. He calls his story "When Promises Outrun Production."

What has fascinated economists in their studies of the Island are its three peculiar characteristics. First, population remains forever constant at 100. Second, only food must be produced; nature provides all other necessities. Third, the Islanders never save; without savings and investment, worker productivity never improves.

From the beginning, these conditions produced a simple economic system. Each of the 100 inhabitants needed 18 ounces of rice per day for survival, and each worker could produce exactly 2 ounces of rice per hour. Therefore, 9 hours of work per day by all inhabitants would have supplied all food required.

But this was an island with a heart. Although most oldsters perished in the sea, among those who made shore were 10

who were over sixty-five years of age. Without hesitation, the 90 survivors under sixty-five volunteered to do all the work. Ten hours daily of rice growing by each of the 90 would supply the island's total requirement of 1800 ounces. Ninety would produce, 100 would consume, and all would feel secure about eating throughout their lifetime.

This monastic rice-only regime prevailed until it was discovered that a non-nutritional but splendidly intoxicating wine could be produced from an abundant indigenous berry. The good life was quickly redefined. Nine ounces of wine daily per person seemed fitting, and the Islanders committed themselves to the extra work required to ferment this quantity of wine.

Finding that 1 worker could produce 5 ounces of wine per hour, the central planning committee reassigned work loads. Since 900 ounces daily were needed, 15 workers were to produce wine, working 12 hours per day (15 workers × 12 hours × 5 ounces hourly). Seventy-five workers were left for rice production and also worked 12 hours daily to grow the required 1800 ounces per day (75 workers × 12 hours × 2 ounces hourly). All except those of retirement age worked equal hours and all, including those of retirement age, consumed equally. All had equally full stomachs and equally foggy minds.

One evening, after a particularly intensive wine-imbibing session, the planners—better politicians than demographers—voted that all inhabitants reaching sixty-five be forever guaranteed their daily 18 ounces of rice and 9 ounces of wine.

Such a statutory affirmation of present behavior seemed harmless. And there was a psychic dividend: those currently producing could now feel certain that the benefits for them in retirement years would equal the benefits they had provided for current retirees.

Many generations pass. Improved longevity plus a low birth rate has today created an island with 70 producers and 30 retirees. The island still needs 1800 ounces of rice daily for survival of its 100 inhabitants, and that need alone would require all 70 workers to toil almost 13 hours per day.

But if all 70 raised rice, the standard of living of the retirees would be illegally reduced. The statutory obligation to retirees mandates 270 ounces of wine daily (30 retirees × 9 ounces); 4 workers therefore must be assigned to this activity. Working 13½ hours per day, these workers can fulfill promises to the retirees (4 workers × 13½ hours × 5 ounces hourly = 270 ounces). Meanwhile, the remaining 66 workers can raise the rice required for both workers and retirees in slightly over 13½ hours of daily work (66 workers × 13$\frac{16}{25}$ hours × 2 ounces hourly = 1800 ounces).

This schedule will leave the working force subsisting on rice alone, forgoing their former ration of wine. Even so, those 70 workers will have to work about 13 percent longer than in the "90–10" era in order to redeem their pledges to the retirees. Retirees will not be better off than formerly, but workers will be working more and consuming less.

If the producers wish to maintain their own standard of living of rice plus wine, they must work no less than 15$\frac{3}{7}$ hours daily (90 producers × 12 hours = 70 producers × 15$\frac{3}{7}$ hours).

The Static Islanders now have learned that promises regarding future consumption must be constrained by a knowledge of demographics and realistic estimates of future production. If the ratio of retirees to producers increases while worker productivity is static, a guarantee of undiminished consumption for each retiree means all producers either must work harder or reduce their own standard of living. Political rhetoric can ignore that equation but cannot change it.

The only escape from this demographic trap is to increase productivity. However, that would require savings—a concept foreign to our Islanders. How much better it would have been if 85 of the original 90 rice growers had worked slightly longer each day, thereby "saving" the labor of 5 of the more inventive workers, who could have devoted that "invested" labor to the fashioning of farm tools.

That action by the Islanders would have been equivalent to the adoption of a private pension plan. If such a plan, with its compulsory heavy savings component, had been utilized in-

stead of the no-savings governmental transfer plan, gain would have fed upon gain.

The regular commitment of "investment" labor would have generated progressively better rice-producing and wine-fermenting equipment, allowing greater output per hour. Labor thereby released from farming would soon have been producing goods previously unthought of. All the Islanders, including retirees, would have had far more product to consume and producers would have been working shorter, rather than longer, hours.

But if that is the way the residents had operated, of course, they wouldn't be known as the Static Islanders.

Let's bid adieu to these economically illiterate Islanders and look at a really advanced civilization—our own.

Our U.S. ratio of Social Security transferees to producing Social Security transferors is about 25/75, up from 10/90 in the mid-1950s. You can take your pick from projections, but the probabilities are high that the Static Islanders' 30/70 ratio will be far exceeded on our own much larger island in the next half century. With demographics working against us, our hope must lie in productivity gains—and in the savings and investment that will generate them.

Originally, all was peaches and cream. When, through Social Security statutes, politicians initially promise Paul a bright economic lifetime from the future production of Peter, Paul feels richer while Peter feels nothing (he may not even be born). The PNP (psychic national product) increases while the RNP (real national product) is unchanged. Just as in embezzlement, one party becomes wealthier while the other is not aware of his impoverishment. Such temporary illusions regarding aggregate wealth understandably produce euphoria. Euphoria, in turn, produces votes. But neither an illusion nor euphoria can produce rice.

As demographic trends grind away, either (1) productivity must rise significantly, (2) producers must lose economic ground, or (3) retiree promises must be modified. Congress must soon face its ultimate nightmare: talking to Peter and Paul simultaneously.

In an era of corporate downsizing and job insecurity, many Americans, worried about flat wages and the next layoff, ask: What's the point of boosting productivity if good jobs are hard to find—and easy to lose? Shouldn't policymakers be at least as concerned about employment—and especially high-paying employment—as about improving productivity growth?

Of course they should. But most economists agree that the creation of good jobs goes hand in hand with higher rates of productivity growth—and, furthermore, that the means to the two ends are the same: a higher rate of capital formation. This in turn presupposes more investment in plant and equipment to allow workers to do their jobs more efficiently and (increasingly important) more investment in the skills of workers themselves. "Lifelong learning and training" and "portable skills" may sound like today's clichés. In fact, they are today's economic imperatives.

Over the short run, productivity gains may show up in higher profits but not in higher wages. This, say some observers, is what is happening now, in the 1990s. Perhaps, though, the criticism is exaggerated. As we shall see, much of the recent improvement in productivity is illusory,* and illusory productivity gains don't translate into real wage gains. It's also true that productivity improvements make certain jobs obsolete—an inevitable part of the dynamic of modern capitalism that is sometimes called creative destruction. It may be no consolation to displaced workers that over the long run the jobs that are lost today will be replaced with better-paying jobs tomorrow. At the beginning of the twentieth century, tens of thousands of blacksmiths lost good

---

* Many of my friends in industry find it hard to reconcile the low official productivity statistics with their own experience of greater efficiency and major cost reductions. It is true that there have been significant productivity improvements in manufacturing and that these are continuing. However, only 15 percent of workers today are in the manufacturing sector; nearly 80 percent are in services, and here productivity has hardly grown at all.

jobs—but not all went on to have successful careers and earn higher wages as auto mechanics. Even so, productivity gains can help. To the extent that the economy is growing and we have our fiscal affairs in order, we will be better able to invest in retraining displaced workers.

So we arrive once again at the need to raise productivity— the one sure way our society has of breaking out of our current vicious spiral of slow growth and diminished expectations. Standard economic theory suggests that my productivity goal would require shifting between 6 and 8 percent of GDP from consumption to savings—thus yielding an overall rate of net national savings and investment of between 10 and 12 percent of GDP, about equal to the current European average and to our own long-term record of the past century. But where will these extra savings—an average of at least $4,500 per U.S. household—come from? Perhaps a third can be obtained by balancing the federal budget and keeping it balanced. The rest will have to come from greater private savings.

5

America's Savings Gap

Thus we come to what we Americans as individuals can and must do for ourselves and our country—that is, ichthyology from the standpoint of the fish. There are four main sources of income for those aged sixty-five and over: (1) continued employment; (2) government benefits; (3) private pension income; and (4) accumulated personal savings. As we shall see, the adequacy of each of these sources is uncertain.

When it comes to our retirement plans, we are a nation in denial.[1] About nine out of ten Boomers say they want to retire at or *before* age sixty-five; about six out of ten want to retire before age sixty. Over two thirds say they will be able to live "where they want" and live "comfortably" throughout their retirement years. A stunning 71 percent expect to maintain in retirement the same or a better standard of living than that which they enjoyed during their working years.

But probe these same Boomers more deeply about their retirement dreams, and most admit they are terrified that neither they nor their government is saving enough. Indeed, the

depth of this anxiety may explain why so many Americans prefer to ignore the issue. Most Boomers say they feel "guilty" about not saving more. Some two thirds confess they've never even calculated how much they should save for their retirement, while an amazing 86 percent believe that "future retirees will face a personal financial crisis twenty years from now." Yet at the same time, they do not expect or even want much from government. Nearly nine out of ten Boomers agree that "the government has made financial promises to [their] generation that it will not be able to keep." For every Boomer who says that government should shoulder the "main responsibility for providing retirement income," five say that individuals should. They will very likely get their wish. From what we have seen in previous chapters, it is obvious that federal benefits (mainly Social Security, Medicare, and Medicaid) are likely to be severely reduced by the time most Boomers retire.

What will replace them? Thirty years ago, experts hoped that private pensions would become a universal supplement to Social Security. But today, less than half of U.S. private-sector workers are covered by pensions. Overall, coverage has been flat since the early 1970s, and in recent years coverage has actually dropped sharply for younger men. The causes have to do with long-term changes in the workforce and in the nature of work itself—part-time work, working at home, multiple careers. Rates of pension coverage have always been highest for full-time career jobs, unionized jobs, and jobs in government and large corporations—in short, for jobs that are becoming increasingly scarce. As for Americans lucky enough to have pensions, they will be surprised, if not seriously disappointed, by how little their plans have set aside for them: For an average-earning workers with thirty years of service, the typical defined benefit plan replaces just one third of preretirement earnings—an amount that is not indexed for inflation.[2]

It is clear, therefore, that retiring Boomers will need to rely heavily on the remaining source of retirement income: *personal savings outside of pensions*. But this source may be the most uncertain of all, for it is questionable whether in recent years the average American household has been saving anything on its own: What one household saves in a bank account or nonpension mutual fund scarcely offsets what another household borrows. Whenever the stock market or housing prices rise, many households may feel that they're saving enough. But our aggregate personal savings rate, except for pensions, is now barely positive.*

Many have argued that the current savings bust is attributable to the passage of so many Baby Boomers through the years of household formation and that savings will turn up again as the Boomers reach the traditionally high-saving middle years. But for this explanation to be valid, the personal savings rate should have bottomed out by the mid-1980s—and climbed back again. Many Boomers have already entered the traditionally peak savings years. But the savings decline persists, contrary to predictions of a demographic reversal.

In 1992, according to Federal Reserve Board data, 43 percent of U.S. families spent more than their income while only 30 percent accumulated assets for long-term savings. In 1993, according to a Merrill Lynch analysis of Census Bureau data, half of all households had less than $1,000 in net financial assets—a figure that had not risen over the past decade, even in nominal dollars. Among adults in their late fifties, the age at which workers are staring directly at retirement, me-

---

* As defined in the National Income and Product Accounts, "personal savings" includes both employer pension contributions and what families save on their own. Total personal savings has averaged 4.9 percent of disposable income thus far in the 1990s. Excluding pensions, however, the personal savings rate is much lower—just 1 to 2 percent in the late 1980s and early 1990s, the most recent period for which data are available. See *Who Will Pay for Your Retirement? The Looming Crisis* (Committee for Economic Development, 1995), page 20.

dian savings are still shy of $10,000.[3] Even the optimists admit that a bleak future awaits the estimated *one third of all Boomers who are expected neither to accumulate financial assets nor to receive a private pension.* Among these will be many of today's burgeoning number of divorced and single mothers, who have well-below-average incomes and few opportunities to save—and who, of course, are less likely than married couples to belong to a household with at least one pension.

The Baby Boom is the best-educated, most-sophisticated, most-traveled generation in our history. That it fails to grasp its predicament is shocking proof of the depth of our denial.

The economist and pension expert Douglas Bernheim concludes that Boomers on average must *triple* their current savings rates if they want to enjoy an undiminished living standard in retirement. And if one assumes that Social Security benefits will be reduced by 35 percent (which seems more than likely, if not inevitable), then Boomers will have to *quintuple* today's savings rates![4] A thought-provoking 1995 study by the Committee for Economic Development, *Who Will Pay for Your Retirement? The Looming Crisis,* comes to a similarly stark conclusion.

If the promise of late-in-life government benefits helped to suppress private savings in the past, the growing expectation of cuts in government benefits may help to boost private savings in the future. Though economic theorists debate the point, people do take government subsidies into account when deciding how much to save. By thirteen to one, households say that they would save more if they *knew* that future Social Security benefits were going to be cut.[5] *This is yet one more reason why Congress must act now to clarify what Social Security will and will not be able to deliver.*

Finally, there remains the prospect of inheritance, that magical cure-all for any generation's retirement worries. Boomers have recently been cheered by a spate of upbeat sto-

ries about the "$10-trillion inheritance boom" that today's affluent seniors are expected to pass on. These Boomers may not have noticed the bumper stickers one sees in resort areas frequented by seniors: I'M SPENDING MY CHILDREN'S INHERITANCE. But even if the hoped-for handoff happens, there's a problem. Because this wealth will be highly concentrated among relatively few families—what Donald Trump calls the Lucky Sperm Club—bequests that may *average* as much as $90,000 per Boomer will amount to only about $30,000 for the *median* Boomer. Muffy and Duffy and their pals will do fine. But for most of this generation, the typical inheritance will just about cover the costs of settling Dad's estate and paying off a few last medical bills.

In a recent study, Public Agenda found that only 20 percent of U.S. households are "planners" who deliberately save toward a quantitative goal.[6] The rest—"strugglers," "impulsives," and "deniers"—leave their future more or less to fate. We must remember that Americans are constantly bombarded by advertising that urges them to borrow and spend— and have been indoctrinated to believe that reducing consumption is bad for the economy. Sixty percent of the respondents in the Public Agenda study said they had received six or more credit card applications in the past year. Although most respondents acknowledged that they had ample room to cut back on household spending, few said they planned to. For example, 68 percent indicated they could save by eating out less often—while only 18 percent indicated that they would likely do so. Younger Americans must understand that a great change in savings behavior is required—but that this change will not be unbearable *if they start now.* Thanks to compound interest, even modest sacrifices count. A recent study by *Fortune* magazine found that if a couple at age forty decides to go out to dinner and a movie only twice a month instead of four times—and puts the $150 monthly savings into a 401(k) plan—they will net $169,500 for their retire-

ment at sixty-five. Paying off credit card bills when they first come in instead of incurring finance charges yields another $121,400.[7]

There are of course millions of Americans who never go out to dinner at $75 a pop—and for many of these families, saving $150 a month is simply an impossible dream. But if most Boomers don't start saving at least something personally for their retirement and if government doesn't act soon to reform entitlements and encourage pensions, their golden years will be nothing like the leisure they expect. In *The Retirement Myth,* Craig Karpel warns that the generation we met in the 1980s as yuppies may reappear around 2020 as "dumpies"—destitute, unprepared, mature people wandering the streets with signs: WILL WORK FOR MEDICINE.

Why have we failed so miserably to prepare for this approaching demographic challenge? Why are we saving less when common sense tells us that an aging society should save more?

One way to answer this question is to reverse it: Why did "this new man, this American"—so optimistic, so full of enterprise and daring, so convinced that El Dorado lay over the next mountain, as for millions of Americans it actually did— bother to save in the first place? The answer is that for some three centuries the characteristically American faith in luck and pluck was tempered and channeled by ethics of Puritan thrift and individual responsibility inherited from our foreign-born ancestors, whose own lives were circumscribed by scarcity. The thrift ethic taught that providence not only bettered one's worldly lot but improved one's character and brought one closer to God. Meanwhile, the ethic of individual responsibility taught that if you didn't save, you would bear the consequence personally. The spendthrift who hit bottom could apologize to his family, implore his neighbors, or beg from strangers—but would have no claim on the public purse.

Thus was a youthful America able to achieve overall rates of savings that were at least as high as those of any other country until the Civil War—and considerably higher during the sixty years after Appomattox. From the time Whitman wrote "O Youth!" to the teeming westward-bound pioneers to the 1920s, when America "roared" with young barnstormers, the U.S. net national savings rate averaged over 12 percent of GDP, a third higher than Germany's and about twice as high as Japan's. Whenever we borrowed heavily from abroad (as we did on occasion, mainly to build railroads and steel plants), we did so only because our lofty savings rate could not match our even loftier investment needs.

After the Great Depression, our savings performance revived, from the 1940s through the early 1970s, to adequate but no longer exceptional levels. Then came the long and fateful slide. Today, Americans are world famous for their welcome but reckless consumption and for their ingenious means of diverting income (through fiscal deficits, home equity loans, no-money-down mortgages, and unfunded benefit liabilities) to the present. Americans have more credit cards (over a billion) than the rest of the world's population combined. But we trail every other industrial nation in the share of economic output devoted to public or private investment.

Why did we abandon our habits of thrift and personal responsibility without putting other constraints in their place? Why did we decide instead to "have it all—and have it now"? Why did whatever hindered instant gratification become irksome, unreasonable, and even anti-American?

The U.S. as a nation of savers: once the world leader, now the world's leading laggard.

Ranking of average annual savings rates*

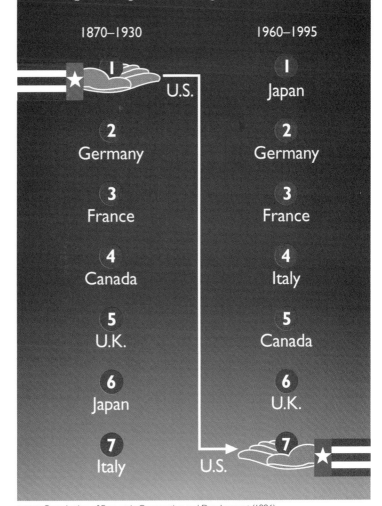

1870–1930	1960–1995
1 U.S.	1 Japan
2 Germany	2 Germany
3 France	3 France
4 Canada	4 Italy
5 U.K.	5 Canada
6 Japan	6 U.K.
7 Italy	7 U.S.

SOURCE: Organization of Economic Cooperation and Development (1996)
*Net national savings as a share of net national product among the "big seven" industrial countries.

6

From the World's
Biggest Saver to the World's
Biggest Consumer

Given the awesome challenge we face, why are we paralyzed? Why do we prefer escapist myths and false promises when so many of us, to judge by the polls, know that we're in serious trouble?

The America I grew up in took a balanced budget for granted. My immigrant father, with only a fourth-grade education, knew what many of us seem to have forgotten today: that building a better future for our children and grandchildren means saving for their future.

America has indeed changed greatly over the past half century:

- From the world's biggest saver to the world's biggest consumer
- From the world's largest creditor to the world's largest debtor
- From a country that sometimes borrowed from abroad, mainly to fund investment, to one that consistently borrows much larger amounts, mainly for consumption

- From a country whose rates of productivity and income growth were the highest of all industrial nations to a country whose rates are among the lowest
- From a country whose bank-vault government saved for our common future to a country whose vending-machine government underwrites consumption for entitled interest groups, each pursuing its private goals
- From a country that invested in its children to one that borrows from its children
- From a country whose political system had the discipline to say no to deficit spending to one that has become addicted to deficit spending—even if it means borrowing on a scale that would have terrified the parents and grandparents of today's leaders

We are no longer the highly purposeful society we once were, a society that knew the future it wanted and was prepared to pay for it. We have instead become a choiceless society, a society that no longer confronts the tough trade-offs between today's consumption and tomorrow's higher living standards. This collective decision not to choose is one of the most fateful decisions Americans have ever made.

We did not deliberately choose deficits and slow growth over a secure future for ourselves and our children. We lost our economic way inadvertently, without consciously making the serious choices that faced us, largely because politicians and the media were afraid to put these choices before us realistically, afraid that if they leveled with us, we would vote against them or turn to a happier channel.

Part of the problem was our unrealistic belief in our own powers: Because we invented the atomic bomb, eradicated polio, and flew to the moon, we decided we could do *everything* at once—and so lost our historic capacity to distinguish necessity from desire, what we have to do from what we want to do. How did this happen? How did we lose our ability to

make the choices that directly affect our economic future—and thus our entire future?

Why did my generation permit this great shift in our national character? How, when, and why did we begin to ignore our common future? Why did we subordinate our long-term national needs to our immediate cravings? How, in a few short decades, did we forget the fundamental lesson of two centuries of American history: that ensuring prosperity tomorrow means giving something up today? How did we become a choiceless society?

Of course, we had always been an unusual society—one which had enjoyed a long history of rapid economic growth unparalleled in any other society the world had ever seen. But until the 1940s, few of us took this unprecedented prosperity for granted. We knew that our collective wealth was not freely given but the result of our collective efforts and that thrift was essential to our continued good fortune.

Perhaps we first began to lose sight of these connections when the Great Depression challenged our most basic economic assumptions, including the principle that public budgets must be balanced. Although few people today think of Roosevelt as a crusader for fiscal balance, he often spoke passionately of eliminating the deficit as soon as the emergency of the Depression had passed, and in January 1937 he told Congress that the final steps toward restoring economic health should be a balanced budget and the replacement of government-stimulated employment by private-sector job growth. But when his abrupt attempt to cut the deficit tumbled the economy into a new recession, he lost the courage of his earlier convictions.* John Maynard Keynes, who himself

---

* Today, policy makers are much better able to gauge the risk of recession by tracking a host of "leading and lagging" indicators—from unemployment claims to "consumer expectations." Even so, it is possible for precipitous tax hikes or spending cuts to trigger an economic contraction. This is why it's essential that any plan to balance the budget be phased in gradually and provide

had originally supported budget restraint, wrote to Roosevelt in 1938, urging him not to worry about a balanced budget but instead to keep stimulating consumer demand. And thereafter, that's the direction that Roosevelt's policies took.

Although it took another twenty-five years before mainstream economists (much less the public) accepted deficit spending as an institutionalized force, Keynes and his followers took FDR's 1937 debacle as proof that the prevailing wisdom about fiscal discipline was wrong. While not denying the crucial importance of savings and investment to productivity and income growth, they stressed that it was consumer demand that ruled the business cycle and that, as necessary, government must prop this up through deficit spending. Over time, the idea that the road to riches lay in this direction came to seem increasingly benign.

This emphasis on consumption took a brief intermission during World War II. But if the new consumerism was respectfully quiescent during the war—as Americans agreed to accept gas rationing and sugar shortages for the common good—it came roaring back as soon as the war was over.

Before long, politicians of both parties learned that the surest way to get re-elected was to give the voters whatever they wanted—in other words, buy now, pay later. This road to our current debacle was traveled by majorities in both parties until the failed policies of the 1980s once again brought us face to face with the fundamental linkage between long-term economic outputs and inputs. Our future prosperity, however, was in jeopardy long before the Reagan administration enormously compounded the federal deficit. In the end, it is both the "welfare-state liberals" and the "supply-side conservatives" to whom we owe our choiceless America, for in the decades that preceded the "supply-side" revolution it

---

incentives that ensure that investment spending accelerates at least as fast as consumption spending slows.

was Democratic opinion leaders who had first persuaded the public to regard the budget and tax code as the means to cost-free consumption.

Our tilt toward choicelessness accelerated soon after World War II. America's industrial plant was undamaged. Indeed, it had been greatly strengthened by the innovations, investments, and incentives of our extraordinary wartime effort. I vividly recall FDR in his fireside chats spurring us on to one almighty production goal after another—fifty thousand planes one day, one hundred thousand tanks another. We always seemed to reach, and even exceed, his goals.

Small wonder that we concluded that *we* alone had won the war. Eventually, I learned that others had a very different view. In 1972, while I was representing our government in negotiations with the Soviet Union on trade and lend-lease payments, General Secretary Leonid Brezhnev took me aside for a rare private discussion. As we looked out over the terrace of his luxurious Black Sea resort home with its Olympic-size indoor-outdoor swimming pool, he grasped my arm, looked me squarely in the eye, and with his voice shaking, said: "Does your President understand that while you ask for cold-cash interest payments on World War II lend-lease and the money we borrowed from you to fight the war, we have already paid far, far more with the blood of twenty-one million Russian lives?" That's seventy times the number of Americans who lost their lives in battle in World War II!

Not only did we believe that we alone had won the war, but our possession of the world's only atomic weapons only added to our pride. With our industrial plant intact and growing and our technological leadership assured in virtually every field, competitive advantage was not something we had to strive for. It was a given. Meanwhile, competing countries seeking to rebuild their cities and their economies had to rally public consensus behind strategies of national sacrifice.

Japan's rise to superpower status was aided by the common

view of its people that it was a humble little island with little food, few resources, and even fewer friends. The Japanese knew they had no alternative but to rebuild their capital stock by investing heavily, which meant saving heavily. This Japanese idea of putting the national interest first, enhanced by such incentives as zero taxes on personal savings up to substantial levels, spawned what became the world's highest-saving, highest-investing economy and our chief foreign competition.

Germany, meanwhile, was fearful of repeating its *own* economic and political history. Its post-war leaders were determined never again to allow the economic collapse that helped give rise to Nazi triumphs, especially the runaway inflation which caused German prices from the summer of 1922 through the end of 1923 to rise over *1 trillion* percent—so that a loaf of bread cost 450 billion marks, up from less than a third of a mark before World War I.

I remember hearing former West German Chancellor Willy Brandt describe how, as a child, he stuffed his family's lifetime savings into bags and took them to the local orphanage, where they were used to start a fire to keep the children warm. "You Americans simply have never experienced the hell that can take place in a country if it doesn't get inflation under control," Brandt said. "It is what brought us Adolf Hitler. It's what transformed, in a hideous way, our entire values and society." After World War II, Germany was committed to high savings, high investment, high productivity, and low interest rates for fear of repeating its catastrophic history.

Thus, Japan and Germany, two very different countries, avoided the pitfalls of extreme Keynesianism and forged, from their deeply painful political experiences, their own brands of future-oriented, pro-producer economies. Both of them did it the old-fashioned way.

We Americans, however, recalling the terrible experience of the 1930s, decided to encourage consumption and build a

demand-side economy. We succeeded—all too well—as we turned our Yankee ingenuity to pioneering increasingly imaginative ways to consume wealth.

As we glorified consumption, we penalized savers by subsidizing government-guaranteed mortgages and by enacting tax breaks for debt, especially unlimited tax deductibility for mortgage interest. Soon we boasted that American home buyers could put a nickel on the dollar down as equity while the Japanese, a nation of savers, often put a third to a half down on their homes! Until the 1980s, the interest on consumer borrowing for practically everything Americans bought was fully tax deductible—a tax-law provision unheard of in other industrial countries. In turn, saved income was subjected to double taxation. First, the income itself is taxed, and then the interest and dividends on the savings are also taxed. We even called income from savings and investment "unearned," much to the astonishment of our trading partners. When I was Secretary of Commerce, I recall being asked more than once by the Japanese Minister of Finance to explain why we put the highest taxes on what we called unearned income. "We have always assumed that income from savings was the most earned of all. It is hard work to save, don't you think?" No wonder Japan became the producer society and we became the consumer society.

Consumption was not encouraged by tax incentives alone. It was reinforced by our media and in our schools. American networks offered unlimited commercial television while schools were less demanding than those in our competitor nations. My wife, Joan Ganz Cooney, co-founder of the Children's Television Workshop and originator of *Sesame Street*, has always been appalled by our laissez-faire attitude toward what television offers our children. "The United States," she tells me, is "the only country in the world that permitted the available VHF channels to be dedicated 100 percent to commercial interests, with virtually no regulation of the networks

and very weak, very loose, very minor, intermittent regulation of local stations or of the number of commercials aimed at children." The message of commercial television is instant gratification—unbalanced for the most part by any call for long-term thinking or for making difficult trade-offs between what you have now and what you can have later. When my own children were growing up, their Saturday-morning television was an endless stream of cartoons and commercials, all telling them to "buy now." (In turn, one of my clearest memories of my own youth is that of the inevitable birthday present: a small metal barrel with a slot in the top—a "gift" from a local S&L—in which my brother and I were expected to save our pennies, nickels, and dimes. My parents assumed that we would make regular trips to this local S&L and deposit these savings for our future.)

Fast economic growth in the post-war years facilitated the American shift to consumption and choicelessness. During the 1950s and 1960s, real take-home pay increased at a yearly rate of 2.5 percent while productivity growth averaged 2.3 percent per year. Within twenty years, real GDP (that is, GDP measured after inflation) doubled. By the mid-1960s, Americans came to assume that effortless economic growth would continue indefinitely.

Meanwhile, economists and social commentators encouraged these limitless expectations. In the late 1960s, Congress listened to expert witnesses testify that accelerating affluence would, by 1985, translate into a twenty-two-hour work week or, alternatively, retirement at age thirty-eight.[1] David Riesman, author of the best-selling *The Lonely Crowd,* which was read by a generation of college students, declared that "the problem of production had been solved" and that now we were "moving into the frontiers of consumption." Stuart Chase, another popular writer, advised us to "cash in on the triumph of our thrift." William Baumol wrote that "in our

economy, by and large, the future can be left to take care of itself." John Kenneth Galbraith, in his best-seller *The Affluent Society,* assured us that we had entered an era of guaranteed plenty and that the consumption and distribution of wealth, not its creation, had become our main economic challenge. Affluence, in a word, was our manifest destiny, and it had arrived.

The buoyant mood of these times is summed up in a now-classic *Newsweek* column by economist Paul Samuelson, who cheerfully predicted in 1967 that Social Security could pay generation after generation of retirees huge returns above and beyond their contributions. Samuelson wrote:

> The beauty about social insurance is that it is *actuarially* unsound. Everyone who reaches retirement age is given benefit privileges that far exceed anything he has paid in. And exceed his payments by more than ten times as much (or five times, counting in employer payments)!
>
> How is this possible? It stems from the fact that the national product is growing at compound interest and can be expected to do so for as far ahead as the eye cannot see. Always there are more youths than old folks in a growing population. More important, with real incomes growing at some 3 percent per year, the taxable base upon which benefits rest in any period are [sic] much greater than the taxes paid historically by the generation now retired. . . .
>
> Social Security is squarely based on what has been called the eighth wonder of the world—compound interest. A growing nation is the greatest Ponzi game ever contrived. And that is a fact, not a paradox.[2]

During the five years after Samuelson wrote his *Newsweek* column, Congress persuaded itself to enact massive and permanent benefit-level increases to all Social Security recipients, rich and poor alike, whether or not they had "earned" the in-

creases through their prior contributions and without asking how younger Americans would be able to pay for them. During those boom years, Americans came to believe that any combination of national goals could be achieved without strain, that our resources were limitless, and that success would be effortless.

We were very wrong. Beginning in the late 1960s, life expectancy at age sixty-five began rising faster than anyone had thought possible. Birth rates fell and never returned to their earlier Boom levels. Beginning in 1973, as we have seen, real growth in wages and in GDP per worker unexpectedly fell sharply while national savings rates sank in tandem, a decline that persists to this day. Benefit promises that had once seemed so affordable soon loomed like Stonehenge over every budget negotiation.

John F. Kennedy's inaugural address memorably embodies the spirit of the 1960s, with all its limitless expectations: "Let every nation know, whether it wishes us well or ill, that we shall pay any price, bear any burden, meet any hardship, support any friend, oppose any foe to assure the survival and the success of liberty." And Kennedy meant it. Soon American forces were plunging into conflicts in remote corners of the world. We did not ask if U.S. involvement in Laos or Vietnam or Cuba was worth the cost, for after all, our President had declared we could afford "any price." Any price? Any burden? Fitting slogans, perhaps, for a nation engaged in total war—but dangerous ones for a nation ready to abandon realistic resource trade-offs. Listening to this "we-can-do-everything" message, perhaps a few Americans felt premonitions of trouble to come. But once the business cycle began revving up late in Kennedy's presidency, most of us forgot such worries. The stodgy Ike years were over. A nation taking "longer strides" (as Kennedy put it)—ready to police the world, guarantee affluence, cure poverty, build monorails, and fly to the moon—was about to get moving again.

Over the last thirty years, benefits paid to middle-class retirees have grown much faster than inflation, population, and GDP.

Growth of non-means-tested entitlements* compared with changes in prices, population, and GDP

Actual spending in FY 1995
$644 billion

Total needed in FY 1995 to keep pace with growth of GDP
$325 billion

Total needed in FY 1995 to keep pace with inflation and population growth
$191 billion

Total needed in FY 1995 to keep pace with inflation since 1965
$143 billion

Actual spending in FY 1965
$31 billion

SOURCE: Congressional Budget Office (1995) and author's calculations
*Non-means-tested entitlements include Social Security, Medicare, federal pensions, farm aid, certain types of veterans' benefits, and other smaller programs that do not look at income in determining eligibility.

Once again, America's leading academics helped out. For several years, the team of "New Economists" that Kennedy had brought with him to the White House had been advocating deliberate budget deficits as a cure for recession. But the message propounded by these academics did not sit well with public opinion. Unreasonably—or so it seemed to the professors—most Americans still distrusted government debt in any form. (Back then, believe it or not, many business groups actually opposed Kennedy's investment tax credit as fiscally irresponsible.) In response, the New Economists organized an educational campaign aimed at ridding the public of its "irrational" Puritan ethic, as they called it. By the time LBJ was in the White House and our 1960s boom was well under way, their new gospel had won America over. Good times were here to stay. Good-bye, Puritan ethic. Hello, go-go sixties.

When Lyndon Johnson assumed office, U.S. GDP was projected to soar to such unimaginable heights by the end of the century that it seemed practically *immoral* not to ask much wealthier future generations to share some of their inevitable riches with those of us living in the (comparatively impoverished) present. Richard Nixon later confided to me that far more than morality was involved. According to Nixon, LBJ was so obsessed with the Ivy League Kennedyites that he was going to outdo them as a liberal in domestic policy innovations.

Thus, LBJ chose to finance his wars against the Communists in Southeast Asia and against poverty at home without raising taxes. Some of his economic advisors, fearful of the inflationary effects of military expenditures that were growing at nearly 20 percent per year, proposed a surtax. But Johnson had no intention of risking his popularity. A proposal to hike taxes, he knew, would force Congress and the public to choose between escalating the war in Vietnam and going ahead full speed with the Great Society and its sweeping expansion of entitlement programs. With the help of

some hasty accounting changes*—and inflation—LBJ was determined to pursue both courses simultaneously. "Guns and butter." We didn't ask which, and we got both. By the end of the decade, vast new initiatives—some stillborn and others ultimately enacted—rose up in spectacular variety: Model Cities (the number of cities started at 7 but soon became 150), Volunteers in Service to America (VISTA), Community Action, the Comprehensive Employment and Training Act (CETA), the Older Americans Act, Medicaid, and Medicare were among the more memorable.

Wilbur Cohen, LBJ's Secretary of Health, Education, and Welfare, came to Johnson with a proposal for a 10 percent across-the-board hike in Social Security benefits. According to Cohen, Johnson replied, "Come on, Wilbur, you can do better than that!" But the most profligate expansion of entitlements was Medicare. When the Medicare bill was being debated by Congress in 1965, Johnson asked about its cost and was told $500 million (that's right, *million,* not *billion*). "Only $500 million," Johnson snapped back, "Get it out."[3] Today—thirty-one years later—the size of Medicare is nearly four hundred times that original estimate. In fiscal year 1996, Medicare will cost $196 *billion*—and it grows by some $20 *billion* each year.

Medicare was a prime example of choicelessness. When Congress debated the pros and cons of various health-benefit programs for the elderly in the spring and summer of 1965, the idea of financing such a program except by open-ended

---

* Among other things, LBJ pushed through a change in the budget law moving Social Security "on-budget." The change itself was sensible. Like any other spending program, Social Security consumes tax dollars that might instead be spent on other public purposes. It most definitely should be counted as part of our "unified" or "consolidated" budget. But the timing of the change was political. It allowed LBJ to cover up a deficit with a Social Security surplus in fiscal year 1969—the last time we ever balanced the budget.

fee-for-service reimbursement was never seriously considered. One reason was that few legislators at the time had the slightest inkling what Medicare would cost a couple of decades down the road. Another reason was the implacable hostility of the American Medical Association and the American Hospital Association to any form of "socialized medicine" that impinged on the "freedom" of their members to treat any beneficiary or charge for their services in their customary manner. The proponents of guaranteed health care for the elderly worried that the AMA might rally enough support to block Medicare—or that health-care providers would wreck it by organized resistance (such as a boycott of beneficiaries).

Medicare's reimbursement policy was thus the result of what critics have called a great bribe. Legislators got what they wanted: acceptance of Medicare by the medical profession. And doctors and hospitals got what they wanted: freedom to practice medicine in return for public money just as they had always practiced it in return for private money. Once again, the answer to "which?" was "both."

Perhaps we reached the critical turning point in 1965, when Medicaid and both parts of Medicare were founded. Or between 1967 and 1972, when Congress enacted a series of across-the-board hikes that raised Social Security benefits by 72 percent over only five years. Or during the next four years, when Congress finally opened the floodgates on federal benefits, which fully doubled over the course of a single (Nixon-Ford) administration with hardly a word of public debate.

Social Security had been born in the Great Depression as a social and political response to a severe economic free fall that profoundly frightened the American people. From 1929 to 1933, real GDP fell by one-third and the New York Stock Exchange plummeted by three quarters; from 1932 to 1935, unemployment averaged over 22 percent. The idea of Social Security, according to FDR, was to give "some measure of

protection to the average citizen . . . against poverty-ridden old age."[4] By the 1970s, that original vision of a floor of protection had been all but forgotten. Social Security was now becoming a massive and indiscriminate middle-class welfare program.

"What is clear is that the revolution of rising expectations, which has been the chief feature of Western society in the past 25 years, is being transformed into a revolution of rising entitlements for the next 25," declared sociologist Daniel Bell in 1976.[5] In concept, these entitlements were supposed to "insure" Americans of all ages against economic vicissitudes. In practice, the benefits were funneled almost entirely to the elderly. It was expected that younger Americans would inherit a prosperous future without lifting a finger. They had youth on their side. Only the old needed government assistance to enjoy the harvest of a Promised Land.

In these same years, America saw the beginning of a sad social and political transformation. Three presidencies in a row were destroyed: Kennedy's, Johnson's, and Nixon's. The assassinations of John Kennedy, Bobby Kennedy, and Martin Luther King, plus Watergate, might have been enough in themselves to cause Americans to lose faith in public institutions. But in my view, Vietnam did even more damage. It did not escape the attention of many, and certainly not America's disadvantaged, that the affluent could avoid the draft while the poor could not. The fact that so many of the poor were minorities only made the injustice more flagrant.

The war's multiple cultural and social shocks greatly eroded our common bonds of citizenship—our "sense of the platoon"—and so, I believe, contributed to the breakdown of trust in our public institutions while encouraging Americans to think in terms of "me" instead of "us." We seemed to be saying, "Don't be a sucker. Grab it before someone else does. There's plenty, and besides, you deserve it." Soon the commitment to the national interest that had long animated

this country gave way before aggressive special-interest organizations.

This pluralist self-indulgence forced our political system to extremes. Though American politics typically avoids ideologies of left and right, the center was steadily becoming incoherent, a collection of intensely parochial and self-interested groups. The historic ability of political parties to mediate among diverse interests and forge unified coalitions declined as groups now petitioned for their own benefit. Political energies in America coursed through ever narrower channels. Deep loyalties often developed around single social issues—clean air, women's rights, abortion, the nuclear freeze, food labeling, school prayer, save the porpoises, and so on. Many of these special interests campaigned relentlessly for federal funds, which contributed further to the growth of consumption at the expense of investment. But since there were no special interests to campaign for posterity, the next generation was left to take care of itself.

From this evolving—or devolving—political culture came our entitlement revolution. Farmers, textile companies, auto unions, weapons contractors, civil servants, military pensioners, S&L depositors, and Social Security retirees—you name the group—all felt they had a right to some pre-arranged award, regardless of what the economy could afford. The budget and the tax system became largely a means of paying benefits to those groups most successful at voicing their grievances and claims. Production was taken for granted, even though by the early 1970s productivity growth was beginning to decline and foreign competition was intensifying. Ensuring one's own share of the national consumption pie became the central political concern.

That was perhaps the beginning of what Robert Hughes writes about in the *Culture of Complaint* and of what Arthur Schlesinger laments in *The Disuniting of America*—a balkanization of society so extreme that claims of victimization and

redress have now come to replace the common good as our idea of citizenship. Many of the new rights Americans have asserted since the 1960s—above all, civil rights—addressed real and painful wrongs that had long festered in our society. The problem is that many of those with grievances to redress were concerned not with asserting long overdue constitutional and political rights but with staking claims to "their" shares of a beleaguered national budget. As for those who made the claims, they were not just—or even primarily—the disadvantaged but a very broad spectrum of America's middle class. We thus came to accept a nonsensical notion: universal entitlements. If we are all victims, the unspoken reasoning goes, we all deserve to be compensated. In effect, all Americans demanded to be put on welfare.

This entitlement revolution swiftly entrenched itself. Each benefit program acquired and nurtured its own "iron triangle," a public, bureaucratic, and congressional constituency which protected the program and assured its continuous expansion with a kind of "what's next?" mentality. Between 1965 and 1981, the number of publicly paid staffers per U.S. senator climbed from sixteen to thirty-six; the number per U.S. representative, from nine to seventeen. In 1971, only five state governments had D.C. offices. By 1982, thirty-four did. From 1973 to 1993, the number of trade and professional associations with offices in the Washington, D.C., area doubled—from 1,128 to 2,325. Meanwhile, the number of lawyers at work in the capital also doubled, from 15,501 (in 1970) to 32,114 (in 1988).

As each of our nonpoverty benefit programs acquired a voter constituency, along with its corresponding bureaucratic and congressional constituencies, those who needed public help most—especially the poor and the young—were less adept at pushing to the front of the line. And since those who wanted something concrete from government were well organized and vocal while those who would benefit from future-

looking public policies were a vast, unorganized, and silent majority, the interests of posterity were sacrificed to the demands of the here and now.

I once asked the cartoonist Saul Steinberg how he might paint this new America as seen from Washington—a parallel to his famous picture of a New Yorker's vision of the world. In the foreground, we would see as giants the dozens of organizations, claiming a combined membership of one hundred million, that protect entitlements for today's retired and elderly Americans. Still prominent—but just a little further in the distance—we would find the hundreds of other agriculture, real estate, health-care, labor, industry, and Wall Street lobbies that also champion the rights of middle- and upper-income Americans to publicly subsidized consumption.

But what about the background of Steinberg's picture? There, barely visible, we would find the young working families who must foot the bill for these entitlements. Along with them, but only as specks of dust on our map, we might also catch a glimpse of America's children and grandchildren—those who will inherit the posterity we are so thoughtlessly neglecting.

America's mindless descent from an endowment ethic to an entitlement ethic was nowhere more evident than in the adoption in the early 1970s of 100 percent cost-of-living adjustments (COLAs) for Social Security. At the time, I served on Richard Nixon's staff and was surprised to find that no one in the White House seemed to consider automatic indexing of entitlements to be a critical fiscal decision. Yet over the last decade alone (from 1986 to 1995), the 100 percent COLAs on Social Security, federal pensions, and other entitlements have added over $100 billion to our *annual* budget and over $525 billion to cumulative federal spending. Over the next five years, COLAs will add roughly another $200 billion to cumulative federal spending.[6] Needless to say, workers' wages are not indexed automatically for inflation;

nor, for that matter, are the overwhelming majority of private pensions. (Indeed, I know of no major company whose pensions are 100 percent COLA indexed.)

The estimable Wilbur Mills was then the sensible and enormously influential chairman of the Ways and Means Committee, a man to be taken seriously by the White House, particularly when he announced his candidacy for President. When Mills spoke, especially on Social Security and tax matters, Washington listened. Mills was the key player in Congress's 1972 decision to enact *both* automatic 100 percent COLAs and a 20 percent across-the-board benefit hike. His reckless enthusiasm for these benefit expansions shows what presidential ambitions can do to otherwise sensible people.

The White House reaction to these extravagant proposals was entirely political. As far as I know, our domestic economic staff never seriously analyzed the cost of the future COLA increases. I *do* recall, however, Nixon's Chief of Staff, Bob Haldeman, walking into a meeting with a yellow legal pad of notes from his regular meeting with the President. For starters, he asked what we thought of putting the American flag, which the Republicans had appropriated as their symbol, on the generous new benefit checks. He then wanted to know whether we thought the President should send out a personally signed notice with all the checks, which were to be mailed just after the 20 percent benefit hike went into effect, and just before the 1972 election.

The Democratic Congress denied Nixon credit by swiftly barring the kind of notice Haldeman mentioned. But the benefit liberalizations themselves became law. Indeed, after a rushed debate during the summer of 1972, the vote in favor of a 20 percent benefit hike *plus* automatic COLAs was overwhelmingly in favor (302 to 35 in the House, 82 to 4 in the Senate). The conservatives rationalized their vote on COLAs by saying that they would *restrict* future Social Security increases to the rate of inflation. The liberals said COLAs

would ensure that future benefits increased *at least* at the rate of inflation. Here, too, the answer to the question "which?" was "both." Years later, Nixon told me that COLAs were probably his worst fiscal mistake. I agree.

But why not? In the early 1960s, federal civilian and military retirees had been granted 100 percent COLAs. The pot was further sweetened in 1965 and again in 1969 by offering them twice-a-year indexing plus an entirely gratuitous 1 percent "kicker" to their annual benefits. When a few lonely critics pointed out that this treatment was vastly more generous than that provided by any private pension plan, Congress sanctimoniously declared that the federal government should be a "model employer"—as if marble bathrooms in Senate office buildings ought to shame all Americans into fixing up their own in similar style. Since we found it easy to be so generous with federal employees—with virtually no discussion of the liabilities to be borne by future taxpayers—why not up the ante with Social Security as well? So, with fulsome pronouncements about the "courage" of Congress, the 1972 Social Security amendments were signed into law by lopsided majorities.

On the subject of federal pensions, I speak with some experience. In 1975, I served as Chairman of President Ford's Commission on Executive, Legislative, and Judicial Salaries, charged with, among other things, reviewing the appropriateness of civil service compensation. The federal witnesses we interviewed were happy to compare the "take-home pay" of federal and private-sector workers—since this was the principal cash outlay that showed up in the annual budget and was also (they thought) the area where federal compensation looked worst relative to private-sector compensation. But as soon as I inquired about the rest of the federal worker-compensation package—the generous vacation and sick pay, the comprehensive health benefits, the very lenient disability policy (one in four federal pensioners was "disabled"), and

especially the extravagant retirement age and other pension-benefit provisions—the witnesses hedged. Well, they said, it wasn't "customary" to compare such things. Several years later, the Grace Commission confirmed our finding that these nonpay fringes, taken together, cost roughly four times more as a share of payroll in the federal government than in a typical private-sector corporation.[7] Nowhere, of course, does the federal budget acknowledge this, let alone account for what this *total* compensation package will cost future taxpayers.

The passage in 1972 of automatic indexing and the huge increases in Social Security benefits it generated were a historic disaster. Shortly after the COLAs were enacted, a sequence of events occurred that might have made us think twice had they happened a year or so earlier—an oil-import embargo, accelerating inflation, a devastating recession, and a slowdown in productivity growth. But it was too late! Entitlement spending exploded as a share of GDP. Along with this unintended economic consequence, there was a political consequence as well. By sheltering retirees from the decline in real family income experienced by many younger Americans, we effectively insulated our most active category of voters—the elderly—from the economic realities of post-1973 America.

Until the 1970s, most federal spending was discretionary and unindexed, and Congress still functioned under the strong presumption that dollars spent should come from revenue, not from borrowing. Large deficits were unlikely to occur because there were so many corrective options available, both in spending and in taxing. We eliminated the spending rule in the early 1970s by making most nonpoverty benefit programs "nondiscretionary"—in other words, automatic, inflation-proof entitlements. In the early 1980s, the taxing rule was also eliminated when the Reagan administration embraced the hijinks of supply-side economists.

Thus, our federal deficit became no one's responsibility. The main items in the budget, politicians could now claim

with a straight face, were no longer subject to control: They grew automatically. They were, after all, "nondiscretionary." The central problem became the inability of both parties to admit that we cannot afford the growing cost of what they pretend we cannot control.

By the time Jimmy Carter arrived at the White House in 1977, the deficit genie was already out of the bottle. But it was not just entitlements that were to blame: Exploding energy prices, soaring interest rates, and inflationary fears created their own mayhem. When Carter entered office, he inherited a $74-billion deficit, the result of our worst postwar recession. In 1980, the year he lost to Reagan, he was saddled with another $74-billion deficit, another recession, and a terrifying new bout of inflation. I recall a meeting with Carter and congressional Democrats at which everyone seemed anguished at the prospect of such large deficits. They hadn't yet heard the motto of the 1980s: "Don't Worry. Be Happy."

After a decade of shattered expectations, America seemed ready for radical political change. Anyone over the age of thirty-five can easily recall the desperate state of the U.S. economy at the end of the Carter years: stagnant real wages, plunging rates of savings and investment, inflation in double digits, and a prime rate soaring past 20 percent. It is no exaggeration to say that by 1980 we were bewildered and frightened. Along with millions of others who voted for Ronald Reagan in 1980, I, too, cast my ballot for a new administration, hoping that it would help us achieve high savings, high investment, and high productivity along with reduced government spending, balanced budgets, and trade surpluses.

Instead, Reagan gave us a spectacular consumption boom financed by foreign borrowing and cuts in private investment, with debt-financed hikes in public spending and huge balance-of-payments deficits. Candidate Reagan had reviled

tax-and-spend Democrats; President Reagan gave us a borrow-and-spend administration, a feel-good decade in which we could have it all—without the bother of actually producing it. "Entitled" Americans grabbed the goodies as fast as ever while the White House assured us that government was nowhere in sight, that free lunches were gone for good, and that a self-reliant private sector was paying the bills.

The supply-siders claimed publicly that their Kemp-Roth tax cut would lower federal taxes by about $1 trillion over the next decade. But by the time the bill landed on President Reagan's desk, it had been decorated with so many bright and shiny tax favors that it took professional accounting firms to keep track of them. The favors included much-liberalized investment depreciation, tax-free savings certificates, special write-offs for trucking companies suffering the trauma of deregulation, big pension-plan write-offs for the upper income brackets (Keoghs), plus tax benefits to farmers, tax breaks for mass-transit systems, tax exemptions for citizens living overseas, major exemptions of estates from federal inheritance taxes, and Employee Stock Ownership Plans (ESOPs). Some of the tax favors may have been legitimate savings and investment incentives, but many others were gifts to special interests. Whatever the case, such distinctions were lost in the rush to pass out the goodies.

How did this wild logrolling go out of control? According to my colleague David Stockman—who, as Director of the Office of Management and Budget, was present at the creation of the Reagan revolution—the supply-side doctrine had the unintended effect of starting a bidding war. "And once the war started," writes Stockman in his memoir, *The Triumph of Politics*, "we became ensnared in its logic. If it was logic, it was that of the alcoholic: One more couldn't hurt, given all that had gone down already."[8] Stockman then describes how "everyone was accusing everyone else of greed,

and in the same breath shouting 'What's in it for me?' " At a White House strategy meeting, Stockman says, Minority Whip Trent Lott summed up the mood: "Everybody else is getting theirs; it's time we got ours."

Stockman's memoir tells us that by the time Washington's tax-cutting party was over, "nearly a trillion dollars in tax revenue had to be spent on the business coalition plan and the congressional ornaments in order to pass a supply-side tax reduction for individuals costing almost an equal amount." In the words of Democratic Congressman David Obey, as Stockman reports them, it would probably have been "cheaper if we gave everyone in the country three wishes." But neoconservative ideologues like Irving Kristol were tireless in broadcasting a more appealing message to Republicans. Stockman sums up the message this way: "Don't cut spending, it's bad politics. Don't raise taxes, its bad politics. Don't worry, $200 billion deficits are nothing to fear because they'll go away on their own."

Stockman bottom-lines this "poker game of calling and raising," as House Majority Leader Jim Wright called it, in one devastating statistical table. "The smoking gun is on line *six*. It shows that had taxes not been raised after the 1981 tax cut, this year (1986) we would be collecting only 16.9 *percent* of GNP in taxes. Built-in spending amounts to about 24 percent of GNP. What kind of crackpot theory says the federal government can issue new bonds in the amount of 7 percent of GNP each and every year and not ruin the economy?" As for the American future, Stockman says that there didn't seem to be much point squandering "a lot of political capital solving some other guy's problem in 2010"—which is the best description I've heard of the White House mood in the crucial, early Reagan years.

Yes, it's true that during the Johnson, Nixon, Ford, and Carter presidencies we added some $500 billion to the public debt and lost sight of the vital trade-offs which the present

owes the future. But during the Reagan and Bush presidencies, we added another $2.5 *trillion!**

There were, of course, opportunities to return to earth, but under Reagan and Bush they were either muffed or ignored as politically suicidal. One such opportunity arose in May 1985, soon after Reagan's second inauguration. During the previous year's "Morning in America" campaign, the President had insisted that he favored a balanced budget. But he had also made three promises that were irreconcilable with this goal: He would not cut his defense-spending plans, raise taxes, or reduce middle- and upper-income entitlements.

After Reagan's victory, many GOP senatorial leaders decided to confront this fiscal gluttony—which was projected to result in a $240-billion deficit in the coming fiscal year—and recommended a return to conservative basics. Their modest proposals included allowing the defense budget to rise only by the rate of inflation, cutting or eliminating a dozen or so minor domestic programs, and imposing a temporary, one-year freeze on Social Security and federal pension COLAs, those most sacred of all cows. All this huffing and puffing still left the projected budget deficit at just under $200 billion. Pete Wilson was called in from the hospital and arrived in a wheelchair to set up a 49–49 vote that Vice President George Bush broke in favor of the Republican proposal. Meanwhile, the Democratically controlled House passed a plan that would have cut the defense budget more severely but eliminated the COLA freeze and most of the other domestic budget savings. The President invited the congressional leaders to a White House cocktail session to resolve the differences. Speaker Tip O'Neill and President Reagan took a walk on the South Lawn. When they returned, O'Neill had

---

* The incremental interest on that additional debt will add about $160 billion to the fiscal year 1996 deficit. Without that extra interest, the deficit would now be about $10 billion instead of $170 billion. Had our public debt merely grown at the rate of GDP since 1980, the 1996 deficit would be about $60 billion.

agreed to restore the defense cuts, and Reagan had agreed to leave the COLAs untouched. So they remain to this day, even when there is persuasive evidence that the current COLA overstates inflation—in other words, that a 100 percent COLA gives retirees an unintended pay raise at a time when taxpaying workers are getting no raises at all.

Senate Republicans felt betrayed by Reagan's overnight reversal, which left them in the awkward position of having to explain to their constituents why they had proposed benefit cuts that their own President didn't think were necessary. In the next election, the Republicans lost eight Senate seats along with their Senate majority. Thereafter, budget negotiations on Capitol Hill became nickel-and-dime skirmishes over very narrow terrain. U.S. fiscal policy was in gridlock.

Just how great the political toxicity of COLA reform is was again brought home to me when I visited the office of Texas Congressman Kent Hance. A Democratic fiscal conservative (a so-called boll weevil), Hance had supported the indexing of income tax brackets to stop inflation-driven tax increases and put a cap on federal revenues. But he had opposed symmetrical reform on the spending side and especially opposed cutting my personal *bête noire,* the automatic 100 percent COLAs. The Congressman and I talked about the threat of runaway entitlement spending to the living standards of tomorrow's workers—and, in particular, the role of these COLAs in inflating benefit costs. As we were wrapping up our discussion, Congressman Hance asked his aide to bring in the letters from constituents who opposed even the most trivial modification of COLA indexing. "You mean all of them?" the aide gasped and, when Hance said yes, brought in a huge stack of letters and telegrams. The Congressman then said, "I wonder if you could now bring in to Mr. Peterson the letters and wires that favor the kind of cutbacks he is proposing." "But Congressman," the aide exclaimed, "we never get letters like that."

I got more firsthand experience of the senior lobby power when I saw how easily it sabotaged the November 1987 budget summit that followed the October 1987 stock market crash. During the early stages of the summit, which was called to arrange a compromise that would begin to reduce the federal deficit, the latest advertisement of the Bipartisan Budget Appeal, a kind of lobby for the future I had organized with the support of five former Secretaries of the Treasury, was prominently displayed in the conferees' working chambers. The message of the advertisement was that the economy was in long-term trouble, and the trouble would get markedly worse unless we moved quickly to control entitlements and reduce the deficit. But as the deliberations were winding to a close, *The Washington Post* reported that the conferees received a videocassette from Congressman Claude Pepper, the indefatigable champion of the elderly, in which he warned of a roll-call vote that would identify anyone in Congress who dared support entitlement cuts. Pepper's video intimated that anyone favoring entitlement reform would be punished by millions of "gray lobby" voters come the 1988 elections. By the time the tape was over, the Budget Appeal's advertisement was removed. "Thereafter," one of the participants later reported, "it was back to politics as usual."

By the mid-1980s, as public spending reached record highs and net savings fell to record lows, it should have been obvious to everyone that despite all the talk of a supply-side revolution, we were actually consuming and borrowing more than ever. But when Senator Pete Domenici pleaded with the President and his advisors to scale back the defense increases and kill the third year of the tax cut, they told him to "get on the team." As the author of "Morning in America" and the host of the debt party, Ronald Reagan should also have led the cleanup party. Instead, he ended his days in office as the most profligate demand-side Keynesian in American history.

The economics of the New Right has been the politics of short-term pleasure and wanton consumption—the "we can always grow out of it," or "deficits don't matter," or "not in a recession," or "not in an election year" nonsense that finally severed the historic American link between present and future in determining public policy. The problem was not only the absurd promise of the Laffer curve, the premise on which supply-side theory was based, that across-the-board tax cuts would so stimulate the economy as to generate higher tax revenues even at much reduced tax rates. There were also the deep cuts in the poverty program and investment corners of the budget, the tacit approval of vast increases in "middle-class" entitlements, and above all, the refusal to take the ominous deficit issue directly to the public.

In 1981, at a meeting of the *Wall Street Journal* editorial board—the unofficial spokespeople for the new administration—I was told that, in effect, my thinking was linear, uncreative, and wrong. Obviously, I did not understand the psychological power of "expectations" of economic growth to turn dreams into reality. I replied that the new Reagan program would shortchange our future if we actually carried it out but that it was so top-heavy with consumption that it would probably self-destruct in short order. I was right about the outcome but wrong about the timing. Something unexpected intervened—something that allowed America to create its make-believe 1960s-style economic boom on borrowed money. That something was debt—and, in particular, foreign debt—mountains of debt created with an abandon unprecedented in our history.

And what did this debt buy us? A boost in private and public consumption that our economy could not otherwise afford. The setbacks of the 1970s suddenly seemed behind us. From vacations on plastic to no-money-down homes, from imported luxury autos to refloated missile-armed battleships, from Day-Glo Keds that cost $100 a pair to redundant CAT

scans that cost $1,000 a minute—Americans once again became convinced that we could "have it all" and "have it now."

To be sure, supercharging the economy did bring some real advantages, the most important of which was to allow the Fed to clamp down hard on inflation—the only policy during the Reagan era that seriously tested our threshold of pain—without triggering an even worse recession than the one we actually experienced in 1982 and 1983. Indirectly and inadvertently, Reaganomics also helped spur a rise in productivity in manufacturing—the one sector of the economy where productivity has risen above the low-growth norm of the past twenty-five years. Scourged by a soaring dollar (itself the result of historically high real interest rates), starved by rising capital costs, forced to fire managerial as well as production workers in droves, U.S. manufacturers producing everything from machine tools to perfume were pushed to the brink. Some went over. But many have come back alive—and not just alive but more efficient and competitive.

The initial aim of the Reagan administration was to improve the critical long-term investment inputs to our economy. Yet suddenly, we started hearing that short-term indicators, such as this year's GDP growth, were the true measure of our long-term economic fortunes. It didn't matter that this growth was mostly due to the huge number of Baby Boomers and first-time women job seekers entering the labor market, not to increases in per worker output and incomes. We were also told that our declining savings rates were a blessing—a sign of confident prosperity which indicated that Americans now took wealth for granted and assumed we would soon become still wealthier. The same logic was applied to our mountains of foreign debt. Since the eagerness of foreigners to invest here meant that our economy was robust and dynamic, why worry about the future bills?

In the end, the debt-driven consumption of the 1980s severely damaged both our economic prospects and our ability

to think clearly about them, for we ended up believing that cost-free prosperity had arrived for good and that no tough choices had to be made even though productivity happened to be growing *more* slowly than before. In other words, our attitude toward the economy in the 1980s underwent a transformation similar to that of our attitudes toward our cultural and social institutions in the 1960s and 1970s: We "let it all hang out" without a thought for tomorrow. After all, if self-actualization—a fancy way of saying self-indulgence—is the key to happiness in our private lives, then maybe the same is true in our public lives. Why deprive ourselves? Why not enjoy another tax cut?

Now the party is over. It is the Morning After in America, and the smile buttons have all but disappeared. What remain are the unpaid bills and a weakened economy. Ex-yuppies are thinking about cutting up their credit cards and staying home for dinner. Department store ads now promote "extra value" and "back to the simple life." Born-again Democratic budget cutters are suddenly pinching pennies while only a ragged remnant of unreformed supply-siders look back with nostalgia to the 1980s—a decade in which the real household income of most Americans under age forty-five actually declined. The world's greatest experiment ever in debt-financed economic stimulus is ending—or so one hopes.

We are now in a corner from which there are no pleasant exits. Perhaps, with members of both parties talking about balancing the budget, we are beginning to face reality. But as I write, there is, so far, little more than talk. The America that conquered the Great Depression in four years and fought and won World War II in four more years is still not ready to legislate the sacrifices required to balance the budget in seven years.

7

America's
Denial Syndrome

"How *specifically* would you constrain them? Who gives up what?" These were the final questions I put to Joseph Perkins, Vice President of the American Association of Retired Persons (AARP), when he appeared in December of 1994 before President Clinton's Bipartisan Commission on Entitlement and Tax Reform, better known as the Kerrey-Danforth Commission after the two senators who chaired it. I had just reminded Mr. Perkins that the commission's interim report (which received one "nay" and thirty "ayes," including the votes of all congressional members) had concluded that unless current tax and spending policies are changed, projected benefit outlays for just five entitlement programs—Social Security, Medicare, Medicaid, and federal civilian and military pensions—would exceed *total federal revenues* by the year 2030. As a commission member, I wanted to ask the representatives of the benefit lobbies who appeared before us just how they planned to avert this catastrophe. Since gargantuan tax hikes were not on the table—Congress and the

President were discussing only tax *cuts*—the only choice seemed to be cutting someone's benefits.

Hence my question to the representative of America's largest retirement lobby: "Who gives up what?" But Mr. Perkins's answer was achingly similar to those offered by the other benefit lobbyists: delay, denial, and diversion. Except for health-care spending, he told me, the entitlement crisis belongs to a distant and merely hypothetical future. As for health care, while he admitted some cuts might be called for, he refused to specify a single one. He did, however, emphasize that any Medicare economizing had to involve "trade-offs"—by which he meant the *addition* of new federal benefits (such as prescription drugs and home care), which he was only too happy to specify. His final remarks implied that his idea of health-care cuts might actually entail an *increase* in total federal outlays relative to current-law projections.

One might dismiss his testimony as the usual special pleading of a lobbyist. (Senator Daniel Patrick Moynihan once quipped to an AARP official who interrupted him: "Madam, please sit down. You are paid to object.") But the problem lies much deeper than that. It isn't just lobbyists like Mr. Perkins who are rearranging the *Titanic*'s deck chairs. The cognitive dissonance I observed in that Capitol Hill hearing room is also reflected in Congress and the nation as a whole. Even when confronted with the difficult facts, we seem incapable of acting on the knowledge.

We saw this happen two years ago in the effort to reform health care. Originally, as President Clinton himself had emphasized, the overriding purpose of reform was to slow the explosion in health-care costs. Yet the longer the issue was debated, the more it became an argument over the merits of "new benefits" versus the dangers of "government control" of the health-care system. By the height of the debate in the summer of 1994, the cost issue was all but forgotten. Just before the Clinton initiative failed, the final Senate bill fea-

tured a "cost-control cap" that sternly assured America that federal health spending would grow no faster under reform than it would have grown without it—no faster, in other words, than what we had originally determined was unsustainable.

The same pattern of denial occurred again during the 1995 debate over a balanced budget amendment (BBA). The original purpose of the BBA was to assure Americans that—after some multiyear grace period—Congress would no longer burden future generations with chronic budget deficits. But as the debate intensified, a bright idea emerged: Let's exempt the Social Security "trust funds" from the BBA requirement, the North Dakota senators suggested. Though the Social Security surplus is due to disappear no later than 2013 and turn into a roaring deficit thereafter, the legislators were not impressed. The proposed Social Security exemption made a joke of the BBA debate, and the amendment crusade quickly fell apart.

The Kerrey-Danforth Commission ended just as ignominiously. Although members had almost unanimously endorsed an interim report that defined the seriousness of the problem, when the time came to endorse a plan to solve it, you could count the ayes on the fingers of a single hand. Perhaps this about face is explained by the 350,000 outraged postcards the commission received from seniors *before* it had even considered a single recommendation.

No matter how clearly the Social Security projections warn us of financial disaster ahead, politicians of both parties are convinced that "middle-class" entitlement programs constitute the third rail of American politics: "Touch it and you're toast." So denial persists and grows. It would be pleasant to blame this denial on Washington and say that the rest of us know better—that all we have to do is elect more principled public servants who will dare to confront the issues. But the problem is interactive. The politicians and the people have

committed themselves to a conspiracy of denial—a conspiracy, alas, whose ultimate victim is our children.

Consider this irony: The public's enthusiasm for cuts in "wasteful" programs is inversely proportional to the cost of those programs. According to one poll, 94 percent of Americans favor cuts in foreign aid, 77 percent favor cuts in public housing, and 75 percent favor cuts in NASA. Yet these programs together make up only about 3 percent of the federal budget.* Meanwhile, though a large majority of Americans insist that the budget should be balanced, only 22 percent favor cuts in Medicare and just 14 percent favor cuts in Social Security. These two programs, together with uncuttable interest costs, make up *half* of the federal budget.

To justify existing benefits (and argue for new benefit expansions), the senior lobby talks as if "old" means "poor." But elderly Americans now have the highest level of per capita financial wealth of any age group—and, counting in-kind income like health benefits, a lower poverty rate than younger adults. On this "total income" basis, Census Bureau data show that the per capita income of households with elderly members is about 60 percent higher than the per capita income of households with children. The average net financial worth of elderly households is three to four times that of households aged thirty-five to forty-four. Back in the early 1960s, the typical seventy-year-old consumed 30 percent *less* (in dollars) than the typical thirty-year-old; today, the typical seventy-year-old consumes nearly 20 percent more.[1]

Although the New Deal originally set up old-age benefits as a "safety net" for the truly needy, today's entitlement system is

---

* Misinformation about the level of foreign aid expenditures is extraordinary. Polls show that the public thinks foreign aid now accounts for 15 percent of federal expenditures and believes that an appropriate level of spending would be 5 percent. In fact, foreign aid currently accounts for just 1 percent of the federal budget! See Steven Kull, "What the Public Knows that Washington Doesn't," *Foreign Policy* (Winter 1995–96).

a well-padded hammock for middle- and upper-class retirees. *One third of Medicare benefits, nearly two fifths of Social Security benefits, and over two thirds of federal pension benefits now go to households with incomes above the U.S. median.*[2] My immigrant father, who taught me by his own example the meaning of the endowment ethic, would have been appalled at our rejection of this principle today. He would have found it positively immoral that young, low-income families are called on to subsidize upper-income elders.

Few Americans, of course, openly defend this arrangement. But for decades, the benefit lobbies have insisted that programs like Social Security and Medicare primarily benefit the poor—while middle- and upper-income Americans have found it convenient to go along with the self-serving myth. It doesn't seem to matter that experts, both liberal and conservative, have long disputed this claim—and that recent data refute it altogether.

Back in the early 1970s, Milton Friedman, the conservative Nobel-laureate economist, made a persuasive case that Social Security is actually a regressive program—since the program's mildly progressive benefit formula compensates neither for its regressive payroll tax nor for the fact that the poor pay taxes over more years (since they tend to start working earlier) and receive benefits over fewer years (since they tend to die earlier).[3] In the 1980s, the celebrated liberal political scientist Mancur Olsen looked over the panoply of American entitlement programs and concluded:

> Most of the redistribution of government is not from upper-income and middle-income people to low-income people. Most of the redistribution of income in fact is from middle-income people to other middle-income people, or from the whole of society to particular groups of rich people, or from one group to another where the groups are distinguished not by one being poor and the other being rich, but only by the fact that some groups are organized and others are not.[4]

Until a few years ago, there was no systematic way to confirm Olsen's critique. Recent data, however, leave the issue beyond doubt: Federal benefits to the affluent are at least as generous as those to the needy.[5] Among Social Security recipients, for instance, those with incomes of $100,000 or more receive, on average, checks that are nearly twice as large as those with incomes of less than $10,000. Even if we add in the cash and in-kind benefits disbursed by all other entitlement programs for which we have income data, including "means-tested" welfare and food stamps, and then average the amounts over all U.S. households, beneficiary and non-beneficiary alike, the result is startling and may help explain why elected officials are so reluctant to touch entitlements. Households with incomes of $100,000 or more received on average about $5,700 in federal entitlements in 1991, slightly more than the $5,600 received on average by households with incomes under $10,000.

Direct federal payments are not the only way the federal government distributes benefits. There are also tax expenditures, such as the home mortgage interest deduction and the tax exclusion for employer-paid health insurance—backdoor entitlements which benefit middle- and upper-income Americans disproportionately. These tax benefits, which are designed to favor certain households regardless of their ability to pay, are the exact equivalent of a government check in the mail. Most tax expenditures are unquestionably regressive: Many poor households cannot qualify for them—and even when they do, what they receive is smaller, relative to their income, than what the affluent get. For example, Congress's Joint Committee on Taxation estimates that in 1993 the average value of the home mortgage deduction for taxpayers with incomes over $200,000 was $4,959—while the same deduction was worth an average of only $478 for taxpayers in the $20,000-to-$30,000 bracket.[6]

When we add the direct benefit outlays to the tax expendi-

The biggest Social Security checks go to the most affluent beneficiaries.

All told, nearly two-fifths of Social Security benefits in 1990 went to households with incomes above $30,000—the U.S. median income that year.

Average Social Security benefit in 1990, by total household income

$5,180

$7,870

$9,210

$9,920

| Under $10,000 | $10,000– $20,000 | $50,000– $100,000 | Over $100,000 |

Total household income

SOURCE: Congressional Budget Office (1994)

tures, an unambiguous picture emerges. On average, households with incomes under $10,000 collected roughly $5,700 in federal benefits in 1991. On average, households with incomes over $100,000 collected $9,300, a distribution of benefits which has nothing to do with economic equality. If the federal government's purpose were to distribute government largesse evenly, it might do better by randomly scattering bushels of hundred-dollar bills by airplane over every city and town.

Fifteen years ago, when Ronald Reagan entered the White House, I hoped that his politically candid talk about cutting the deficit would lead to politically courageous action. But instead, we got the predictable scapegoat. The unworthy poor, we learned, were bankrupting America. Just eliminate the "waste, fraud, and abuse" in our welfare system—all those welfare queens in mink driving Cadillacs and drinking vodka at taxpayers' expense—and a balanced budget would be in reach. The premise, of course, was wrong. Despite cuts in programs for the poorest Americans during the Reagan years, the deficit kept rising.

When Bill Clinton entered the White House, I again hoped that the President would seize the moment, cut the deficit, and boost savings and investment. Instead, Clinton treated us to his own form of scapegoating. This time the poor are not to blame; it is the rich who are not paying their way. To be sure, Clinton may get further with his scapegoat than Reagan got with his. But the truth is that we are all implicated in our budget deficits, our entitlement ethos, and the overall consumption bias in our economy. And all of us, especially the broad middle class, the backbone of America, must now become part of the solution. It does no more good to blame the rich than to blame the poor since both are too few in number to solve what is in fact everyone's problem.

Consider the brute numbers. In 1991, the only year for which comprehensive statistics are available, $270 billion in

direct entitlement benefits (43 percent of the total) went to households with incomes above $30,000—or approximately the national median that year. These households received another $102 billion in back-door tax expenditures (74 percent of the total). This comes to a total of $372 billion—a figure I estimate has since grown in the past five years by one third, to about $500 billion. Yet of the $372 billion in entitlements going to above-median households in 1991, only $5 billion in direct benefits and $10 billion in tax expenditures went to those relatively few Americans with incomes above $200,000. The remaining $357 billion went to the vast middle class.

If we are serious about putting our fiscal house in order, we must come to grips with the Willie Sutton factor. When Sutton, a notorious bank robber, was asked why he robbed banks, he replied, "Because that's where the money is." Neither the poor nor the rich can solve our deficit problem. Only the broad middle class can.

What really is the middle class? Ask any American if he or she is middle class, and the answer will almost always be yes. The truly poor will admit to being lower middle class, and the rich will go along with upper middle class. But few will forthrightly call themselves poor or rich. This characteristically American self-perception reflects our decent desire to live in a basically egalitarian society. But this egalitarianism also allows nonpoor Americans to believe that they deserve universal federal entitlements—much of them windfalls—which are disingenuously called insurance and which beneficiaries mistakenly think of as the payback on their "contributions."

Next, ask any group of Americans to specify the annual income that defines "middle class," and you'll hear responses ranging from, say, $20,000 up to $200,000. But there is a more precise and realistic definition. The median family income in the United States in 1993 was $31,700. If middle class is then narrowly defined as comprising half of all Amer-

The cost of "them"—welfare, foreign aid, and defense—has fallen precipitously.

% of the budget going to defense, foreign aid, and welfare (Aid to Families with Dependent Children)

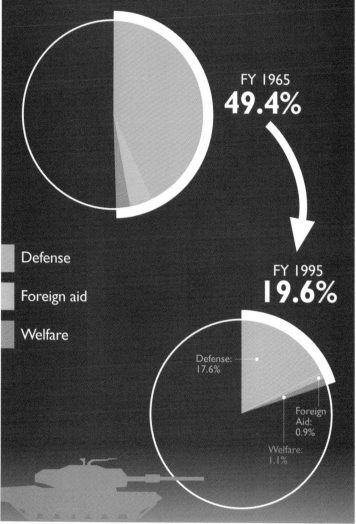

FY 1965
49.4%

FY 1995
19.6%

Defense

Foreign aid

Welfare

Defense: 17.6%

Foreign Aid: 0.9%

Welfare: 1.1%

SOURCE: Office of Management and Budget (1995)

The cost of "us"—the broad middle class—is rising *fast.*

% of the federal budget going to three major "middle-class" entitlements

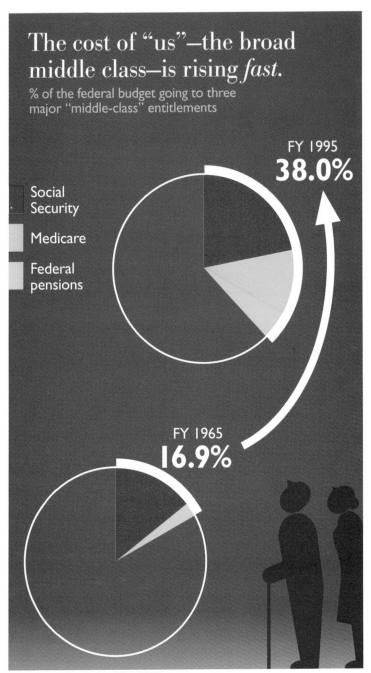

Social Security

Medicare

Federal pensions

FY 1995
38.0%

FY 1965
16.9%

SOURCE: Congressional Budget Office (1995)

ican families equally distributed around that $31,700 family, the statistical middle-class income turns out to range from $14,040 to $55,880.[7]

I have found this exposition to startle those who are new to it. A family with an income of $60,000 often thinks of itself as "just getting by," but it actually stands in the top quarter of American families. A two-earner family with an income of $120,000 may think of itself as "only middle class," but this family stands in the top 5 percent of American families. Those with incomes in excess of $200,000 are a statistical sliver of the population: roughly 1 percent. Yes, this upper 1 percent earns a disproportionate share of U.S. income and owns a disproportionate share of the nation's wealth—which is why I supported President Clinton's higher tax rates for the upper-income brackets. Given this disproportion, these families should certainly be denied their current allotment of entitlement benefits. But the point I am making is that even if we took away all of their benefits ten times over, we would hardly dent the federal deficit.

Middle-class Americans today seem to suffer from what might be called a reverse Lake Wobegon syndrome. As Garrison Keillor fans know, Lake Wobegon is a wonderful fictional place where all the children are above average. But when it comes to incomes, most middle-class Americans, struggling to make ends meet, assume they are below average. Middle-class Americans feel beleaguered—and they are. Even $50,000 a year in household income—well above the median—is hardly easy street when paychecks barely cover the cost of homes, of college educations, and sometimes even of necessities.

Working hard and trying to follow the rules, middle-class Americans have adopted a kind of siege mentality in the face of evaporating expectations about future income growth. This loss of upward mobility has already imposed upon the middle class a de facto and major unplanned sacrifice. Yet

only an organized, planned, and temporary additional sacrifice can reverse this trend, for only if all of us give up something now to reinvest in our collective future can our living standards resume their historic rise. If we simply hunker down to protect what we feel entitled to, our future will grow even bleaker. Diminished expectations are not what America is about. The willingness of middle-class citizens to sacrifice a little today for a better tomorrow is, however, exactly what America *used* to be about and ought to be about once again.

Despite stagnating living standards, the American middle class is still the richest in the world, consuming far more than its counterparts in Europe and Japan—and paying far lower taxes than most. Most Americans think they are overtaxed, but in fact we pay some 10 to 20 percent less of our national income in taxes than citizens pay in most other industrial countries. Although the necessary sacrifices will not be painless, the economic room for sacrifice exists. We lack only the public understanding and political will to see that such sacrifice is in our long-term best interest—indeed, that it may be a matter of national survival.

We can't, of course, ask the middle class alone to sacrifice. The rich must pay their fuller and fairer share. Many who argue that the middle class is already too beleaguered to contribute further stand by silently as the $30,000-a-year middle-class family pays ever-increasing payroll taxes (which typically come to nearly *twice* their income taxes) to subsidize the entitlement benefits of retirees who are getting several times their contributions in Medicare payments (tax free) and who may be earning $1 million or more a year in retirement. This is unconscionable.

But one thing is certain. The numbers simply don't add up without the middle class, which means that everybody except the poor and the near poor must become part of the solution. On the other hand, the sacrifices should be sharply progressive along the income ladder through the middle and upper-

middle classes. By the time we reach the genuine upper class, we should be cutting deeply into tax subsidies and windfall entitlement benefits, which are a disgrace.

The worst aspect of our addiction to entitlements is that it subtly fixes our attention on what we expect to get, not on what we have been given by our predecessors and what we wish to pass on in our turn. It's time for the great American middle class to abandon its entitlement ethic, relearn its endowment ethic, and decide how much to give up today in order to save for the sake of rising living standards tomorrow. The alternative—a stagnating or declining future—is no future at all.

8

Praying for Productivity
and Other Good Things

Of course, there will always be those who claim there really is no problem. Some believe that economic growth will so increase the incomes of future workers as to render any entitlement burden affordable. The only problem with this argument is that it's wrong. Even if productivity growth improves by one third—the assumption in SSA's official intermediate scenario—the rising cost of senior benefits will, as we've seen, cancel out all growth in real after-tax worker earnings over the next half century. Under SSA's high-cost scenario, real worker earnings would suffer a catastrophic decline of 59 percent.

Other counselors of complacency find comfort in the bleak demographic trends themselves. Writing in the *Washington Post*, Richard Leone, President of the Twentieth Century Fund, pronounces the aging of America a nonproblem because the number of children per working-age adult is projected to fall almost as fast as the number of elderly is projected to rise.[1] The result, according to Leone, is that fu-

ture workers will face little or no net new "dependency burden." This is not only untrue but perverse—so perverse that
it's worth quoting at length from The Concord Coalition's response to Leone.

A stable ratio of dependents to workers does *not* mean that
America's aging will impose only a minor extra burden on tomorrow's workers. Leone's demographic numbers alone say
nothing about the vastly greater cost of supporting each senior. At the federal level, the ratio of per capita spending on
the elderly to spending on children is *eleven to one.* Even including state and local spending, and hence the nation's entire
education budget, the ratio is at least three to one and maybe
as high as *five to one* in favor of the elderly. (There are no up-
to-date numbers on state and local spending by age group.)

Yes, families spend a lot of their own money on their kids,
and if we took this into account it would narrow (but not
eliminate) the gap in dependency costs. But why should we? In
our economy, there's an obvious difference between personal
spending and public spending (for one thing, only the latter
runs up the national debt). And in our political system, there's
an obvious difference between compulsory transfers and voluntary giving. Some might argue that personal spending on a
dependent is not really voluntary. But this doesn't wash. Perhaps some people may regard helping out grandma as an
other-than-voluntary burden. But this is not ordinarily the
case with children, since the decision to raise a family is usually a matter of choice.

Then there is the most profound issue of all. To the dependency theorists, any worker income spent on someone other
than oneself is a worker burden—regardless of whether the
transfer (or gift) represents saving for the future or paying off
the past. Leone is perplexed that Americans look forward to
the senior boom with anxiety but didn't consider the 1960s an
era of "deprivation," even though the total demographic dependency ratio was higher in 1960 than it will be in 2030. The
difference is that thirty-five years ago adults were sacrificing

to *build the future* while thirty-five years hence they will be sacrificing to *reward the past.*[2]

H. L. Mencken once quipped, "The prophesying business is like writing fugues; it is fatal to everyone save the man of absolute genius." Since long-term projections are obviously fraught with pitfalls, it's worth asking if there are any favorable trends underway that might mitigate the otherwise bleak forecasts. After looking at the evidence, my advice is: Don't hold your breath. Yes, there are some favorable economic and demographic developments. But even if these pan out, they won't come close to erasing the red ink.

First, consider productivity, which determines real wage growth and hence tomorrow's tax base. Those who preach that high tech will bail us out and that rapid economic growth is assured without saving and investing tell us not to worry: We're in the midst of a productivity revolution. Not quite. For one thing, after the Commerce Department recently updated its methodology, the much touted productivity gains of the 1990s turn out to be just about typical of earlier business-cycle recoveries over the past twenty-five years. For another, the Social Security Administration's official intermediate scenario already presupposes a permanent one-third improvement in productivity over our historical record since 1973. In other words, productivity growth will have to accelerate simply to ensure that the future isn't *worse* than the SSA's already unsustainable projection. It will have to accelerate still more to ensure that things turn out better.

If the productivity revolution won't save us—at least as it is now unfolding—what about the new baby boomlet? It's true that current fertility rates (about 2 to 2.1 lifetime births per woman) are encouraging when compared with the rates of 1.7 to 1.9 recorded during the "birth dearth" of the 1970s and 1980s. But even if these higher rates prove lasting, they won't have much effect on federal revenues until the 2030s—

long after fiscal meltdown is scheduled to occur. Even then, the positive impact will be small. To stabilize the ratio of retirees to workers, U.S. fertility would have to surge to a rate of 3 births per woman or higher—in other words, back to the Baby Boom levels of the 1950s and early 1960s.[3] No one expects this to happen. For one thing, the share of American women who say that a family of four or more children is "ideal" has fallen from nearly 50 percent to about 10 percent since the 1950s. For another, the U.S. fertility rate is already among the highest in the developed world. Average fertility in other major industrial countries is now 1.6. In Germany and Italy, it is 1.3. The forces leading to lower fertility rates—such as safe and widely available birth control technology and the rising share of women who either want to work or must work in order to produce a middle-class family income—are global, and likely to continue.

If not babies, what about immigrants? Isn't importing more young workers a viable solution to our aging problem? Again, not really. Because immigrants too eventually grow old—and thus add to Social Security and Medicare costs, only huge and destabilizing waves of immigration would substantially reduce the burden tomorrow's workers will have to bear. In fact, to cancel out the projected growth in the Social Security payroll tax rate over the next half century, today's level of net immigration would have to roughly quintuple, to about five million a year beginning now. Yet far from being in a mood to reopen Ellis Island, the large majority of Americans want to restrict immigration.

Finally, consider health-care spending. The recent slowdown in medical-*price* inflation (as measured by the Consumer Price Index) encourages optimists to conclude that the market is finally controlling health-care *costs*. Not so. Prices are just one variable in the cost equation, which also depends on the mix and volume of services. What matters are total health-care expenditures, and thus far in the 1990s real

federal health-benefit outlays have not slowed at all. More-over, the official projections *already* assume a dramatic turn-around in recent trends. Over the past quarter century, real Medicare spending per beneficiary has risen at a blistering rate of 5 percent a year, several times faster than real per capita income growth. Over no five-year period since 1970 has real Medicare growth been less than 3 percent. Yet the SSA's official projection assumes that the growth in real per beneficiary Medicare spending will slow to about 1 percent per year by 2020. Incredibly, this projected triumph of cost containment is timed to occur just as aging Baby Boomers vastly increase the demand for every imaginable type of health-care service.

So let's hope—or pray—for productivity gains, higher fer-tility rates, and market-imposed discipline on health-care costs. But let's not forget the "rosy scenarios" of the 1980s that never came true and the fiscal problems we never grew our way out of. Public policy must be based on prudent ex-pectations about the future—and prudence suggests that on our current trajectory the future may be even worse than the official forecasts.

9

Seven Coming
Transformations

Modern Americans are inverse Victorians. The Victorians are famous for their prudishness about sex. But they openly spoke about and planned for their old age and eventual death. A dignified death and a proud cemetery site represented important social values. Their detailed wills were a boon to Britain's legal profession. We are just the opposite: We will talk to just about anyone and say just about anything about our sexual experiences. Yet we deal with aging and mortality as reluctantly as the Victorians dealt with sex.

Because we are still a nation in denial, the scope of the social, cultural, and economic transformation our aging society must now embark on will shock and surprise many of us. "Shake your windows and rattle your doors" is what Bob Dylan wrote about Boomers when they first came of age. This book is about how aging Boomers may once more shake the windows and rattle the doors of this society.

On her deathbed, Gertrude Stein is said to have asked her old friend Alice B. Toklas, "What is the answer?" When Ms. Toklas did not respond, Gertrude then asked, "In that case,

what is the question?" I don't profess to know all the questions, much less the answers. But the fiscal and demographic numbers suggest that the transformation from our still predominantly young society to the much older society of the next century will be among the most fateful America has ever undergone. This transformation will bring profound changes in our expectations about retirement and health care, in our attitude toward America's youth, and in our economic relations with the rest of the world. Let's consider seven of the most important transformations.

1. The Savings Transformation

As I have said, a graying America must balance its public budgets and renew its private thrift. As I have also said, less than half of American workers are now covered by private pension plans, and these are often inadequate. *Apart from pensions,* the *personal* savings rate in the United States is now barely positive. How can we boost private savings when the private savings rate has been falling for a quarter of a century? How can we cut government benefits when, for millions of us, there is nothing to take their place?

Other industrial countries, concerned that their national savings are inadequate to sustain their own aging populations, are coming up with bold solutions. Take Australia, which recently put in place a system of mandatory employer pensions while at the same time means-testing its system of pay-as-you-go government old-age benefits. Under this employer mandate—called the Superannuation Guarantee— employers are required to contribute 9 percent of payroll to workers' retirement accounts. Although employers make the contributions, they are immediately vested and fully portable: Workers can take their savings with them from job to job. In addition, when the system is fully phased in, employees will be required to contribute a further 3 percent of

pay on their own. Up to substantial income levels, the government will match workers' individual contributions, thus yielding a total pension contribution of 15 percent of payroll. Before the system was enacted, only 40 percent of Australian workers had pensions. Today, nearly 90 percent have them. Government actuaries estimate that the new system will ultimately generate an increase in the Australian net national savings rate of 4 percent of GDP.[1]

Even many developing countries, as I pointed out earlier, are taking major steps to prepare for their (still distant) age waves. In Singapore, workers and their employers together are required to contribute 40 percent of pay to worker-owned accounts invested in the Central Provident Fund, the mandatory savings system established in 1955 and thereafter expanded by Lee Kuan Yew, Singapore's venerable Senior Minister. The contributions are tax exempt, the withdrawals are tax exempt, and the total amount of savings is exempt from estate taxes. Singapore's legendary economic performance as one of the original "Tigers," has been largely sustained by this prodigious supply of capital. Meanwhile in Chile—another economic success story—the worker-owned assets in the fifteen-year-old fully funded retirement system total half of GDP.[2]

Singapore established its Central Provident Fund with a clean slate. Chile, on the other hand, had to convert an existing pay-as-you-go social insurance system to a savings-based system. As the first country anywhere in the world to do so, its experience has attracted considerable attention in the United States.

Chile's experiment began in 1981, when its pay-as-you-go retirement system, which had led to soaring tax rates and widespread tax evasion, was closed to all new labor-force entrants. New workers were required to contribute to privately invested personal savings accounts. Current retirees continued to receive benefits under the old system while current

workers could choose to stay or switch. Those who switched were compensated for prior payroll taxes in the form of Recognition Bonds—government IOUs redeemable upon retirement. Twenty-five percent switched in just the first month, and by now 90 percent have chosen the new system.

Contributions to Chile's new funded pension system are set at 10 percent of payroll, plus an additional 3 percent to cover the cost of disability and survivors' benefits. Workers pay these contributions themselves; there are no employer contributions. All pension savings must be invested with one of some twenty publicly regulated (but privately managed) Pension Fund Administration companies. Upon reaching retirement age, participants may purchase an annuity from a private insurance company or make periodic withdrawals from their investment fund. In either case, account balances in excess of the amount needed to pay for a standard pension benefit equal to 70 percent of preretirement earnings can be withdrawn and used for any purpose. The retirement age for men is set at sixty-five and for women at sixty. But these ages are not rigid. Workers can start collecting a pension earlier provided that their accounts contain sufficient savings to fund a benefit equal to 50 percent of their preretirement salary. Moreover, if they choose, "retirees" can continue to work while collecting their full pension benefits; there is no "earnings test" as there is under our Social Security system. The government continues to provide a means-tested floor of protection, which is paid for out of general revenues. But this guaranteed minimum benefit is only payable if and when a low-income worker's personal pension funds have been exhausted. As Joseph Piñera, Chile's former Minister of Labor and Social Welfare, explains, "no one is defined as poor a priori."[3] Except for this floor of protection, retirement benefits are determined solely by an individual's lifetime savings. The Chilean reform thus defuses the potential for intergenera-

tional conflict that is inherent in all pay-as-you-go social insurance systems.

The Chilean reform has certainly been a success so far. Since the system first began to operate, the average real rate of return on investments has been 14 percent per year. Currently, the average retiree receives a pension equal to 78 percent of preretirement earnings; if lump sum withdrawals are included in the calculation, the replacement rate is 84 percent. (By way of comparison, Social Security replaces about 43 percent of an average worker's earnings.) In addition to improving retirement incomes and retirement security, the savings generated by Chile's pension system (the Chilean savings rate is now about one quarter of GDP) helps to explain why the Chilean economy has doubled its real rate of growth to an average of 6.5 percent over the past dozen years, the highest growth rate in Latin America. Meanwhile, since the reform was enacted the unemployment rate in Chile has fallen to just 5 percent.

"Privatization" of Social Security like Chile—or mandatory pensions like Australia—might help shift our economy from consumption to savings. Chile's example in particular is inspiring a large number of reform proposals. Senators Bob Kerrey and Alan Simpson, for example, have sponsored bipartisan legislation to allow workers to deposit 2 percent of payroll, or one-sixth of their FICA taxes, in IRAs. Meanwhile, at least half a dozen think tanks—from the libertarian Cato Institute to the "New Democrat" Progressive Policy Institute—are developing plans of their own. In the spring of 1995, five out of thirteen members of President Clinton's official Social Security Advisory Council endorsed a proposal to shift about half of the current FICA tax into personally owned and privately invested worker accounts. Another two members endorsed a similar but more modest plan.

The problem is that many of these schemes imply that the transition from a pay-as-you-go system to a funded system

will be painless. It won't. Workers would have to save for their own retirement in addition to paying benefits to current retirees—the so-called double-burden problem. If workers are simply allowed to shift their FICA taxes into savings accounts, the resulting increase in the federal deficit will cancel out the increase in private savings dollar for dollar. National savings—and future living standards—will be no better off than they would be if we had never reformed the system.

On this score, Chile enjoyed advantages that we do not. For one thing, Chile was running large budget surpluses when it instituted its new pension plan and so could pay much of the cost of benefits to current retirees from general revenues. Chile was also in the midst of privatizing large state-run industries, which gave it another ready source of funds to cover transition costs. We, of course, are running a budget deficit, not a surplus. Nor, of course, do we have large state-run industries to sell for the benefit of the Treasury. Most important, Chile is much younger than America. Only 6 percent of Chileans are over age sixty-five, while 12 percent of Americans are, which means that retirement costs in Chile can be spread over relatively more taxpayers. Even so, Chile has still incurred a substantial debt for benefits under its old pay-as-you-go system which must someday be paid off. As the Recognition Bonds come due, much of the boost to Chile's savings could be dissipated.

Later, I will propose my own plan for a mandatory system of personally owned and privately invested savings accounts— a plan that honestly confronts these transition issues. There are no free lunches! To save more, we must consume less—at least temporarily. For current retirees, that will mean giving up some of the Social Security benefits they have been promised. For current workers, it will mean setting aside more of their income for retirement savings. The potential opposition to my plan will, of course, be ferocious and can-

not be overcome except by an electorate aware of the price to pay if we do nothing.

Our economy, our tax system, and much of our culture are committed to limitless consumption and to the motto "Buy now, save later"—which in practice means never. In such a climate, how do we build political support for a mandated savings plan—or for other reforms, such as a progressive consumption tax system, that would further encourage thrift? What psychological and cultural arguments can moderate the power of advertising and the many other seductions of our demand-side economy? Americans are now learning how hard it is to convert defense industries to commercial businesses. The transformation from a consumption economy to a savings economy will be vastly more difficult. But we have no choice.

2. The Retirement Transformation

The magic number sixty-five was first chosen as the standard retirement age by Germany's Chancellor Bismarck over a century ago, when life expectancy in Germany was just forty-five. Some statistical wags have computed that to provide comparable retirement protection in the United States today, the Social Security eligibility age would have to be raised to ninety-five. Retirement at age sixty-five is no longer affordable. Moreover, as a growing number of Americans reach their late sixties and seventies in good health and with employable skills, it is no longer enlightened social policy.

Nothing is more likely to promote personal contentment and longevity in old age than productive employment. In fact, the mechanistic division of the life cycle into three boxes—first education, then work, then leisure—is now under attack by virtually the entire gerontology profession. Even prominent senior advocates agree. As Robert Butler, former Director of the National Institute on Aging, puts it, America must

develop a new vision of "productive aging" in which "work expectancy" increases along with life expectancy.[4] We seek satisfying love and sex after sixty—why not satisfying work as well? The old idea of a rocking-chair retirement is dead, and it is time for the idea of an active yet aimless and dependent retirement to die as well.

When a University of Michigan study asked people aged sixty-five and over if they would like to have some sort of paying job, 73 percent said yes. The problem is that today's Social Security and private pension systems make early retirement so attractive that few seniors follow through. As recently as 1950, most men who were physically able worked past the age of sixty-five; a third of those over seventy remained in the labor force. Today, despite longer and healthier lives, a mere 16 percent of elderly men work past the age of sixty-five—a share that has not changed over the past decade.

Most Boomers say they too expect to retire at sixty-five—or earlier. They will not get their wish. The policy question now is whether to raise Social Security's retirement age to sixty-eight, to seventy, or to seventy-two—and when to tell those affected so that they can adjust their plans. We must also change the perverse Social Security incentives that now penalize seniors who remain in (or re-enter) the work force. We must develop private-sector management and training programs to make seniors more attractive employees. And we must revamp traditional career patterns to allow for semi-retirement, phased retirement, and "un-retirement." In the next century, old age will still bring its reward of leisure, but retirement will no longer be the all-or-nothing proposition it is today.

3. The Health Transformation

On the eve of the New Deal, local, state, and federal government combined spent roughly $1 a year on health care for

the typical older American. By 1965, that figure had risen to roughly $100; by 1975, to roughly $1,000; by 1995, to roughly $7,000. Thirty years ago, America spent more on national defense than on health care. By the year 2005, health care is projected to consume 18 percent of GDP, at least five times what we are likely to spend on defense. Compared with the per capita average spent by other industrial countries, the *extra* dollars that we now spend on health care would be enough to *double* our net fixed business investment, *double* our total corporate spending on R&D, *double* our total net additions to public infrastructure, *double* our total federal and state cash benefits for the poor, and *double* our total federal aid to child nutrition and education.[5] Not just double each of these items. Double *all* of them. And that's before the special multipliers of the age wave—especially the huge growth in the numbers of old old most likely to require extensive acute and chronic care—even begin to kick in.

Americans like to believe that high and rising health-care costs are primarily the result of waste, fraud, and abuse. If only we get rid of all the unnecessary tests and treatments, or slash the excessive paperwork, or get tough on Medicaid cheats and profiteering drug companies, then presto, the problem will be solved. But experts know that the real causes are far more intractable: fabulous (and fabulously expensive) new medical technologies, cost-blind benefit and insurance systems that exempt most of us from making meaningful trade-offs, and perhaps most important, our typical American disdain for limits, including the ultimate limit, death itself. Abroad, doctors work within guidelines that balance the health of the patient against the expense of treatment and the probability of its success. In America, whether the condition is trivial or hopeless, we demand the response portrayed on *E/R* and *Chicago Hope:* the intervention of swarms of specialists and the latest technology.

Dan Yankelovich, the dean of U.S. pollsters, tells me that

this spare-no-costs attitude is explained by our view that health care is a "maximum right." No matter what we or society can afford, we believe that everyone always has a right to the very best that medicine has to offer. Yet we regard almost everything else as a "minimum right." Take food, for example. Everyone agrees that it is unconscionable to let people starve on the streets. But when society feeds the poor, we don't have in mind a steak dinner. Nor do we believe that every American deserves a subsidized education at Yale. As real incomes flatten or decline, as family debts rise, and as the job outlook becomes increasingly uncertain, most Americans have become more value conscious than they were during the spendthrift 1980s. But not where health care is concerned.

Hard as it may be to say no, other countries do not switch on multimillion-dollar MRI scanners for routine complaints, or commit terminally ill patients to intensive-care units, or perform heart bypasses on septuagenarians at anywhere near the rates we do. Consider a few examples: The United States has more than seven times as many radiation therapy units and eight times as many MRI units per capita as Canada. We have four and a half times as many open-heart surgery units and three times as many lithotripsy units per capita as Germany.

The challenge in controlling costs is that it's next to impossible to point to medical procedures that are wasteful in the sense that they have absolutely no potential medical benefit. How much, for example, should we spend on tests to avert very low risks, such as colon cancer screening for thirty-five-year-olds? When should we attempt low-probability cures, such as bone marrow transplants? Inevitably, one physician's (or bureaucrat's) notion of waste is another's idea of good medicine. And what may seem like waste for a stranger is a must for a loved one. The Brookings Institution's Director of Economic Studies, Henry Aaron, thus speaks for most thoughtful observers when he writes that "sustained reduc-

tions in the growth of health-care spending can be achieved only if some beneficial care is denied to some people."

A disproportionate share of medical dollars is spent at the near end and at the far end of life, much of it on patients whose chances of survival are remote. Should we spend hundreds of thousands of dollars to save a premature infant whose chance of survival is small—and who in any case is likely to suffer permanent neurological damage and become totally dependent on society? Or should we instead spend that money on prenatal care for scores of women who cannot afford it? According to the C. Everett Koop Institute, founded by the former Surgeon General, "It costs only $900 to provide basic prenatal care, . . . a fraction of what we spend on premature and low-birth-weight babies."

Heroic intervention where the odds of success are small (or nonexistent) is even more costly at the far end of life. Medicare spends nearly 30 percent of its giant budget on patients in their last year of life—often when there is no hope of long-term recovery.[6] As recently as 1950, half of the deaths in New York City occurred at home in bed. Today, 85 percent of New Yorkers die in hospitals—often hooked up to tubes in what amounts to a senseless postponement of death.

Dr. Paul Marks, President of Memorial Sloan-Kettering Cancer Center of New York, has analyzed a number of studies which show that terminally ill patients consume a disproportionate share of hospital resources, owing in part, as he says, to "interventions with high technology medical care which have little or no benefit for the patient." One recurring finding of these studies is that about 5 percent of patients (on average) consume about 20 to 30 percent of total expenditures. Another is that the majority of these high-cost patients die either during hospitalization or shortly after. Dr. Marks believes that we could achieve major savings if we placed limits on this "mindless extravagance" and adds that if we invested a small part of this savings in preventative medicine,

"we would not only save a lot of money but would end up a much healthier nation."

In Europe, intensive-care units, or ICUs—with their expensive high-tech equipment—account for just 1 to 5 percent of all hospital beds. In the United States, they account for 15 to 20 percent. Another difference between ICUs here and abroad, as one expert has observed, is that "the common patient in an ICU in a major U.S. hospital is an 85-year-old whose heart is failing, whose lungs are failing, who is in need of artificial respiration. The patients abroad are different: They are healthier and younger." In England, a neurologist treating an eighty-year-old stroke victim with no significant chance of recovery turns that patient over to a general practitioner, who sends him or her home. Here, that same patient is likely to end his or her days in an ICU as the object of "heroic intervention."

My good friend Dr. Fred Plum, a world-class neurologist, has written about "the uselessness of heroically treating illnesses in which death is inevitable within a matter of days or a very few painful weeks." His conclusions are worth repeating:

> Only a few states have statutes that enable physicians (with family consent) to suspend treatments having no medical benefit. Most states, including New York, limit the futility application to patients who are predicted to die within forty-eight hours. Given present resuscitation equipment, it is almost impossible to predict death with such accuracy unless one withdraws life-supporting machines. Many patients spend pain-racked or machine-supported days of suffering or semi-consciousness before merciful death finally stops the clock and the cost explosion. To achieve the goal of limiting futile care, doctors must be allowed greater discretion in considering further medical care as having no benefit in restoring personality or significantly extending life.[7]

I do not pretend to have all the answers to our health-care crisis. No one does. But I do know there are certain questions

our aging society can no longer avoid. Who decides when government should pay for heroic medical intervention for the burgeoning number of elderly, especially the very old? How do we determine that even if an extra year or two of life is possible, this is not the right social goal to pursue when so many young people lack even basic health insurance? No other aspect of America's age transformation presents such profound ethical questions: Who lives? Who dies? Who decides? Questions like these invoke the dreaded and un-American word—"rationing." But whatever we choose to call it (and whether we let government or private markets do it), rationing is precisely what we must confront.

4. The Education Transformation

Tomorrow's workers will be relatively few, but they will inherit a huge national debt and high and rising payroll taxes. To make matters worse, many more of these future adults than today's adults will have grown up in impoverished and dysfunctional families, neighborhoods, and schools. More than any other industrial nation, we have seeded a poverty-stricken and violent Third World within our First World. According to the Carnegie Corporation, over one third of America's children lack the basic ingredients necessary for school readiness—from physical well-being and language skills to social confidence and maturity.

Since 1973, the real median income of households headed by adults aged sixty-five and over has risen by over 25 percent while the real median income of households under thirty-five has fallen by over 10 percent. Counting all sources of income, poverty in America is three times as likely to afflict the very young as the very old.[8] One third of our children are born out of wedlock, and only a fraction of their fathers are willing to assume legal, financial, and moral responsibility for them. The United States leads the world in life expectancy

at age eighty-five—but comes out worse than almost every industrial country in crime,* infant mortality, marital breakup, drug abuse, child abuse, child poverty, hours of school-assigned homework, functional literacy, educational achievement, and on-the-job investment in the training and retraining of workers. Meanwhile, per capita federal benefits to the elderly tower twelve to one over benefits to children.[9]

Computer literacy is now a requirement for modern workers. Over the past decade, the overall percentage of U.S. workers who directly use computers has roughly doubled, from one-quarter to one-half. But only one out of ten high school dropouts use computers on the job, compared with two out of three college graduates. Workers must now adapt quickly to constantly evolving technologies, management techniques, and production know-how that demand good reading and math skills and the ability to communicate orally and in writing. Can we remain an economic superpower in an increasingly competitive, technological, and information-based global economy when our high school dropout and functional illiteracy rates are the highest in the industrial world?

This is not just a matter of ensuring business profits but of creating good jobs that pay high wages. While the average U.S. real wage has been flat since the early 1970s, this trend actually masks divergent outcomes for different groups of workers. The wages of college graduates have continued to grow (though more slowly than before); the wages of Americans without college degrees have plummeted.

I'm talking here not about physical capital but about human, intellectual, and social capital: the strong family life, work habits, education, and high-tech skills upon which increased productivity ultimately rests. In an economy where

---

* Of all the melancholy statistics on crime in America, one sticks out in my mind: There are now over four times as many Americans serving time in prison as twenty-five years ago.

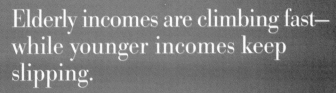

Elderly incomes are climbing fast—while younger incomes keep slipping.

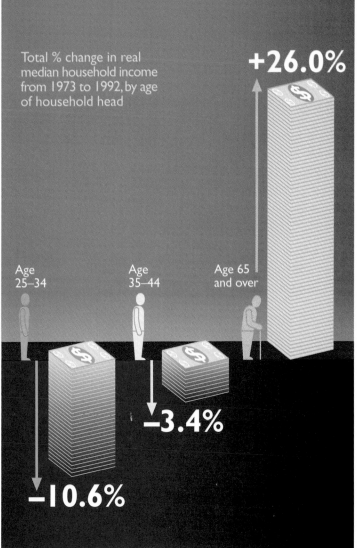

Total % change in real median household income from 1973 to 1992, by age of household head

+26.0%

Age 25–34

Age 35–44

Age 65 and over

−3.4%

−10.6%

SOURCE: Census Bureau (1993)

Young children are three times more likely than the elderly to fall beneath the poverty line.

% of people in poverty in 1992, counting all sources of income*

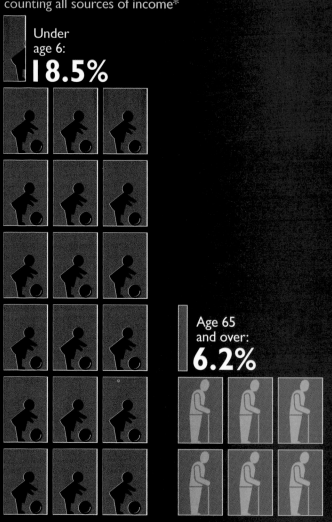

Under age 6:
18.5%

Age 65 and over:
6.2%

SOURCE: Census Bureau (1993)
*In addition to cash, income includes noncash benefits such as Medicare and Medicaid.

What the federal budget spends on each elderly American dwarfs what it spends on each child.

Per capita federal benefit spending in FY 1995, by age group

age 65 and over
$15,701

under age 18
$1,258

SOURCE: House Ways and Means Committee *Green Book* (1993) and author's calculations

each future retiree will depend upon as few as one and a half to two workers for support, self-interest alone demands that today's young be the best-educated, most-skilled, and most-productive workers we have ever had. There is much evidence that formal on-the-job training significantly increases productivity. Yet we invest far less than other industrial countries in worker training. Over two thirds of sixteen- to nineteen-year-old Germans are in apprenticeship programs compared with only a fraction of 1 percent of Americans. Abundant and powerful evidence suggests that early-childhood education also pays off. Why can the French find money for a *universal* child-care benefit while we can't afford to fully fund Head Start?

An aging America will depend on the skills, education, and civic goodwill of its younger generations. How can we invest publicly in America's youth when the effectiveness of most current government training programs is suspect—and when, in any event, even a Democratic President tells us that "the era of big government is over"? How can we motivate employers—whose companies may not capture the payoffs until years later—to invest privately in the training of an increasingly mobile workforce? And how can we motivate employees themselves to take responsibility for their own lifelong learning and training? How, in short, can today's overburdened economy generate the funding and political will to keep Americans and America competitive?

5. The Political Transformation

Washington reacts to the senior lobby with fear and trembling. In the late 1960s, elderly voters began to coalesce around dozens of retirement lobbies—from the Gray Panthers to the National Council of Senior Citizens, from the National Association of Retired Federal Employees and the Retired Officers Association to the National Retired Teachers

Association. Since then, these groups have grown in numbers and wealth. The largest and the best known, of course, is AARP. Its thirty-four million members include half of all Americans over age fifty, which is to say one in every four U.S. registered voters. Its gross income of over $2 billion makes it the largest business in the Washington, D.C., area. Twice the size of the AFL-CIO, AARP has more members than any other voluntary organization in the United States except the Catholic Church. The *AARP Bulletin* has a larger circulation than *Reader's Digest* and *TV Guide*.

The senior lobby is further strengthened by the fact that children can't vote and young adults are less likely to vote than their elders. Today, Americans under thirty-five compose 27 percent of the electorate (but 53 percent of the population) while those over sixty-five compose 20 percent of the electorate (but 12 percent of the population). By the year 2040, assuming voting behavior doesn't change, those shares of the electorate will be 19 percent versus 31 percent.[10] Will an aging America permanently enthrone the senior lobby as an invincible political titan?

Some experts say this won't happen. They argue that organized interest groups remain effective only when they are small enough not to provoke taxpayers to take countermeasures. This is why Milton Friedman and others predict that the senior lobby's long-term prospects are doomed—and that it will have no more success as a political lobby in the twenty-first century than organized farmers had in the nineteenth century, when they composed well over half the population.

This prediction is far too sanguine. Although it is safe to assume that the more senior power grows the more resistance it will encounter, the outcome is far from certain. To avoid political strife between generations, we must reaffirm the traditional ties that unite the interests of different age groups by ensuring that government assists, not replaces, the efforts of family members to care for one another and by giving the

young tangible proof that elders are willing to sacrifice on their behalf.

Singapore's Lee Kuan Yew recently offered two provocative suggestions: that retirees be required to sue their adult children for support before applying for public benefits and that each taxpaying worker be given two votes to balance the organized power of retired seniors. The Lee Plan is not a serious possibility, but it makes a useful point: An aging America must succeed in merging the interests of young and old, for it would be a disaster if they became adversaries.

6. The Global Transformation

I recently asked the head of Japan's central bank why his country has resisted our repeated requests to reduce its budget surplus and stimulate consumer demand. His immediate reply—"because Japan must save so it can afford its coming retirement wave"—serves as a warning that the abundant and relatively inexpensive supply of foreign capital we have been depending on to finance the federal deficit may soon disappear.

Roughly one third of U.S. domestic investment since 1980 has been funded by foreign lenders—which means that we must permanently send part of our national income abroad in the form of interest or dividend payments. The more serious problem, however, is not that this borrowing will continue unabated but that it will slow substantially (or cost much more) as aging populations in other industrial countries consume more of their own national income and savings. If Americans cannot boost their domestic savings rate within the next decade, we may be faced with rising real interest rates, capital rationing, and a further curtailment of domestic investment.

A much more open, fluid, and competitive world economy will be neither kind nor gentle but the harsh enemy of ineffi-

ciency wherever it occurs. Until recently, protected markets permitted us to negotiate costly social bargains for seniors and workers alike. Now, however, serious new competitive pressures—particularly from developing countries—are intruding upon these comfortable arrangements. With corporations downsizing even as the cost of social insurance contracts grows, the affordability of old-age entitlement systems inevitably becomes entangled with concerns over job security. None of the "solutions" to the latter problem is easy or even clear. Protectionism, for example, would offer only a temporary reprieve to the least productive and lowest-paying jobs while jeopardizing jobs in the export sector, which tend to be the most productive, competitive, and highest paid. Massive infrastructure programs, to take another example, can boost short-term job growth. But unless the funds are spent on investments with real economic payoffs, they will not help (and may hurt) long-term productivity growth.

Others suggest that the solution is for corporations to enter a "social responsibility covenant" with workers that would promise improved job security. But this solution, too, is not costless. All other things being equal, the higher costs of guaranteed employment would mean one or more of the following—lower wages, lower profits, higher consumer prices, or less investment. Other more cohesive societies—Japan for example—have been willing to pay one or more of these costs as part of a "lifetime employment contract." Are we?*

---

* Herbert Stein has recently tried to clarify some of the complexities of this issue: "Some people would say that employers have a social responsibility to commit themselves to providing more assured employment. But would this social responsibility extend to paying workers as much as they would get without that commitment? And, if it did, would investors have a social responsibility to provide as much capital and on the same terms as they would without the employment commitment? And would consumers have a social responsibility to buy as much product if the commitment entailed higher prices? And who would have a social responsibility to the people who did not get employed in the first place because it would have entailed too large a commitment? The social responsibility approach draws us into a thicket from which escape is not easy. And the prob-

Then there is the issue of our relation to the less-developed world. When half the population in the United States is over the age of forty, half the population in some emerging markets of Latin America and Asia may still be under twenty-five. Will the current distinction between rich and poor nations come to be seen as a difference between old and young nations? Will the former, mainly in North America and Western Europe, be characterized by creative consumption, short-time horizons, and the defense of the global status quo—while the latter, mainly in Asia and Latin America, become known for energetic investment, long-time horizons, and revolutionary changes in the global balance of power? What happens to the newly democratized economies of the former Soviet bloc if sources of investment capital in Western Europe, North America, and Japan dry up? Or, alternatively, will a high-saving Third World emerge as a major exporter of capital to a low-saving First World in an ironic reversal of the policy recommendations of the 1970s? How will these demographic and economic shifts affect global institutions such as the UN, the Organisation for Economic Co-operation and Development (OECD), and the World Trade Organization? Will they continue to enjoy the public confidence and international support needed to address the myriad challenges posed by the global age wave?

More than ever as our society ages, the problems of the rest of the world will become our problems. Some Americans may be comforted to know that many other industrial nations are aging even faster than we are. Or that, according to economists at the OECD, *the unfunded pension liabilities of these*

---

lem is not made any easier by the suggestion now being floated around that tax benefits be given to corporations that act responsibly as defined by someone (perhaps the Secretary of Labor). To search for ways to improve the conditions of employment is desirable. But before changes are made we should try to consider all their implications—not just the ones that first come to mind and to the headlines." *The Wall Street Journal* (April 14, 1996).

countries' generous public retirement systems are, as a share of GDP, one and one half to two and one half times larger than our own.[11] But think again. Capital markets are no longer local but global. When these unprecedented liabilities come due, the financial shock wave will be registered in New York just as surely as in Bonn or Tokyo.

7. Business Transformations: The Emerging Gray Markets

Some experts believe that Baby Boom retirees, who are destined to live longer and healthier lives than today's seniors, will constitute a booming elder market just as they once constituted a booming youth market. They are half-right. There will be plenty of seniors with money to spend—and many affluent Baby Boomers, as they age, will try to look, act, and feel young. Innovations in cosmetics and cosmetic surgery, elder-friendly exercise equipment, senior fitness centers, high-tech vision and hearing aids, home security systems, specially tailored popular culture and entertainment (including television programming), and lifetime learning—you name it—could all become the foundation of new business empires early in the next century. On the other hand, Cruise-line executives and Sun Belt developers could be in for a sobering surprise. Remember: sooner or later, senior entitlements are bound to be cut. Meanwhile, a majority of Boomers are on track to reach old age with inadequate pensions and meager savings.

Some markets will of course do well in any case. One safe prediction is that aging Baby Boomers will redouble the demand for health-care services. The market for high-tech medicine will continue to expand—though tomorrow's health-care entrepreneurs will doubtless look back with nostalgia on the good old days of cost-plus reimbursement. The greatest payoffs, however, are likely to go to businesses spe-

cializing in *lower-cost, more efficient health care*—from tele-medicine to cost-effective alternatives to nursing home care.

Financial services are also likely to flourish—at least until aging Baby Boomers start cashing out assets en masse. Indeed, if middle-aged seniors-to-be start saving in earnest, and especially if we set up a system of mandatory pension accounts, the entire asset management industry, including retirement and estate planning, will probably experience rapid growth well into the next century. And this brings us to where we started: America's coming savings transformation.

10

Turning America from Consumption and Deficits to Savings and Investment: What Needs to Be Done

It is certainly not my view that America is in decline. But we live in a finite world, in which every desire can't be satisfied and where bad choices lead to tragic outcomes.

America is faced with so many social "crises" it may seem presumptuous to say that the problem of aging deserves our full attention. But let there be no doubt: The implications of aging will dwarf, in sheer economic terms, all our other serious problems, from race to national security. In fact, how we deal with aging may determine how these other issues ultimately play out.

A graying America must now become a saving America, balancing its public budgets and renewing its private thrift. Our political leaders cannot be expected to take this challenge seriously unless we as individuals do so as well. A program of thrift has to work on all fronts—from Congress to the homes of ordinary Americans. Let me suggest some practical steps:

1. Achieve and Guarantee
Long-Term Budget Balance by the Year 2002

Of all our policy choices, none will raise America's national savings rate more quickly and certainly than eliminating our chronic deficits. We should aim *at least* to balance the federal budget—and ideally, we should aim for a surplus.

Reducing the deficit presents economic risks if we simply and suddenly cut government spending. But this is not what I propose. A workable plan must be gradual and provide for budget outlays and tax incentives to promote investment. We cannot merely rely on lower interest rates to ensure that investment purchases accelerate at least as fast as consumer purchases slow. For households to become bigger savers and businesses smarter investors, we must also change perverse tax and benefit policies that discourage thrift and hamper rational investment decisions. In other words, we need a plan that reduces unfunded benefit liabilities and that restructures the tax system to reward saving and investment.

Still, for those who would prefer to do nothing, deficits will always appear the least threatening of evils. Politicians and others who oppose a long-term program to balance the budget invoke the fear of short-term economic collapse and stress the need to bolster confidence among consumers and investors. When an economic recovery is still in its early stages and vulnerable, they warn that balancing the budget over any foreseeable period could dump us back into the last recession. When the economy is at full speed, they say that we must tolerate big deficits so as not to tumble into the *next* recession, and during a recession they insist that deficits are the path to recovery. If the business cycle is not enough, the political election cycle supplies other reasons for inaction, so that there is never a right time to begin balancing the budget.

The reality is just the opposite. We must have a national

commitment to a long-term savings goal not only to achieve future prosperity but to create the consumer and investor confidence to shore up the current economy. Continued failure to address our long-term problem could trigger a financial crisis or a new surge in interest rates, either one of which could cause a recession. On the other hand, a credible plan to balance the budget would boost the economy—if, as most economists, including Fed Chairman Alan Greenspan, believe likely, the markets react to this display of prudence by lowering long-term interest rates by as much as two percentage points. Lower rates will not only encourage investment spending—bolstering employment and GDP growth—but could result in a lower dollar, which would increase exports. Lower rates will also help balance the budget by reducing the cost of debt service. A smaller debt service charge means a smaller deficit—which in turn means still lower interest rates and still smaller deficits.

Some critics concede that a smaller deficit may be advisable but argue that we need not go so far as to close the deficit entirely. Economists disagree, these critics say, on how to measure perfect budget balance. Should accrued obligations to future retirees be included on the federal balance sheet? How should capital expenditures be accounted for? They also stress that many other industrial nations have higher public-sector borrowing rates than we do and yet still enjoy more rapid growth in productivity and living standards. Even Japan ran large deficits for a time during the 1980s. Yes, these critics conclude, perfect budget balance may be optimal. But should we really worry if we remain a bit short of perfection? Is it going to make or break the U.S. economy?

In my opinion, these critics misunderstand both the economic purpose and the political dynamics of deficit reduction. The purpose of balancing the budget is not to placate the god of fiscal probity but to help achieve a substantial rise—roughly 6 to 8 percent of GDP—in an inadequate na-

tional savings rate. Balancing the budget alone will not achieve this result. Such increased national savings will require a large budget surplus and/or a substantial increase in private-sector savings. But actually balancing the budget will surely get us closer to our goal than not quite balancing it.

From the perspective of raising national savings, it doesn't matter how perfect balance is measured—or that some high-growth economies run large deficits. What the critics overlook is that these other economies typically save two to four times more privately than we do and so can afford large public-sector deficits without depriving the private sector of needed investment funds. We can't. Consider: In 1993, Japan had a private-sector savings rate of 21 percent of GDP and a public-sector deficit of 3 percent of GDP—which yields a net national savings rate of 18 percent of GDP. With a private savings rate of 5 percent of GDP and a deficit of 3 percent of GDP that year, our net national savings rate was 2 percent, or *one ninth of Japan's.*

And what about the political dynamics? Former Congressional Budget Office Director Robert Reischauer has compared a budget plan without balance as its clear goal to an Apollo program whose objective is to send a man somewhere into space and then have him return.* Half measures and amorphous goals won't convince most Americans that shared sacrifice is essential. For the politics of deficit reduction to work, our leaders must promise us the moon—and deliver it. In short, we need a political symbol around which the public

---

* "The notion of balance is important primarily because it provides us with a clear and definable destination for our deficit reduction journey. One can't underestimate . . . the importance of having a clear destination when one embarks on a major public sector undertaking. If you think back to the 1960s, I doubt if the space program would have gone too far if President Kennedy had simply asked for the ability to send a man 239,000 miles into space and then have him return. We needed the moon. We needed something out there to go to." Robert Reischauer, paper delivered at The Concord Coalition's annual National Policy Forum (April 13, 1993).

can rally to the cause of fiscal responsibility or, to use today's politically correct formulation, "smaller government." A balanced budget is such a symbol.

Finally, there are some who say that America faces graver economic threats than the deficit and that the cause of balancing the budget is a diversion that will prevent us from addressing our real problems. From the right, we hear that the real problem is slow growth. From the left, we hear that it is stagnant wages and a widening income distribution. Both sides miss the point. Without more savings and investment, we will get neither higher growth nor higher wages and a fairer income distribution. Boosting savings and investment, of course, is what balancing the budget is all about.

I believe that we should achieve budget balance no later than 2002—the date which a bipartisan consensus now endorses, albeit after considerable Republican pressure. The 1996 federal budget deficit is expected to be less than 2 percent of GDP. Over the past few decades, the United States, along with every other major industrial nation, has managed to reduce public-sector deficits by *more* than 2 percent of GDP in *fewer* than seven years. (We did it in the late 1970s and again in the early 1990s.) Moreover, since the federal deficit is projected to start growing rapidly soon after the year 2000, a longer timetable only makes the long-term effort more difficult. The longer we wait, the closer we come to the retirement of the Boomers—with its explosive implications for entitlement spending. Balancing the budget, starting now, is like running to catch a train that's leaving the station. To catch it in two minutes, we will have to run harder than we would have to run to catch it in one—and if we wait too long, we may miss it entirely.

The reforms we enact should, at least provisionally, guarantee long-term budget balance *after* the year 2002, not just a temporary balance *in* 2002. To achieve *permanent* fiscal discipline, I have reluctantly come to believe that our limp

political system requires a balanced budget amendment—one with no exceptions for Social Security or any other special trust fund or "off-budget" expenditure. This amendment would require Congress to maintain a balanced budget over the next fifty years—not just in the current year. Exceptions would be allowed in times of national emergency—whether a major war or a major recession. But an exception would require a 60–40 majority of Congress.

No one advocates amending the Constitution for the sake of the next business cycle or the next decade. But today's federal budget, through entitlement programs, transfers vast sums between generations and makes promises that will burden taxpayers fifty and seventy-five years from now. A balanced budget amendment would force us to confront the long-term problem that we now deny.

In fact, a balanced budget amendment would fundamentally change our entire approach to the federal budget. Instead of guaranteeing a spending program and then hoping we can afford it, we would have to show that we can afford our policy choices based on prudent projections. If things turn out better than anticipated, we could either spend more or cut taxes. A balanced budget amendment also means abandoning phony trust-fund accounting. No longer could we declare Social Security or Medicare solvent by using current cash surpluses that have already been spent to cancel out long-term cash deficits we have no idea how to pay for. The amendment would require us to admit what is already true in practice—that, unless contributions are truly saved, all federal benefits are strictly pay-as-you-go. As senior citizen benefits rise or fall, so will the burden on future taxpayers.

It is not enough, however, to balance the budget over seven years and keep it balanced. Congress should aim for an overall budget *surplus* of perhaps 1 or 2 percent of GDP through the first two decades of the next century, partly to make up for our recent profligacy but, more important, to lay up

stores during the Boomers' peak earning years for the sudden burden that will accompany their retirement.

Or better still, Congress could aim for a somewhat smaller budget surplus but substantially increase spending on targeted public investments in education, worker training (especially computer-related instruction), and research and development—the *human infrastructure* investment that is so essential for an information-age economy but in which we are now deficient. True, genuine public investment is difficult to define. Lest public investment be confused with public pork, a few ground rules are necessary. First, all of this money must go into R&D and physical and human capital formation programs with demonstrated or credible high rates of return. To help ensure this, each proposal for new spending should be accompanied by a "productivity impact statement." Second, no new money is to be spent on investments for which a reliable and near-term private-sector market exists. Government can provide an invaluable service to our economy by funding basic research; it should not be in the business of directly funding and managing commercial development. Finally (and it's worth noting that this is the common practice in Japan), our investment priorities should be ranked *in advance* of their funding by agencies and expert panels acting independently of our elected representatives. The highest priorities would be met first; the lower priorities, as funding allows. Congress would thus be answerable to the electorate not only for what it does fund but also for the worthwhile projects it ignores. Furthermore, with such a system in place, it would be possible, if fiscal stimulus is needed, for Congress to move up new projects according to rational criteria instead of just dishing out pork.

Either way, we would radically change the economic and social function of the federal budget—from a means of leaning on the goodwill of our children to a means of expressing our goodwill toward them, from a means of distributing con-

sumption that divides us as net takers to a means of making investments that unite us as net givers.

2. Reform Entitlement Programs

Trying to balance the budget without reforming entitlements is like trying to clean out the garage without removing the Winnebago. It cannot be done. The needed reforms can be fair, protect the vulnerable, and give individuals and families plenty of time to adjust and prepare. Or they can be draconian. For reform to be humane, we must act now, not when the crisis is upon us, for then the choices will truly be unbearable.

The following seven principles should guide us as we reform entitlements:

Ask for across-the-board sacrifice. Across-the-board sacrifice is fair, fiscally necessary, and politically imperative. Only by asking *all* groups of federal beneficiaries to make meaningful sacrifices can we get the numbers to add up. And only by guaranteeing that the sacrifice is broadly and proportionately shared can we disarm the benefit lobbies: No group can be treated specially, and none can be spared. If older workers are asked to postpone retirement, so too must young professionals sacrifice some of their mortgage interest and health insurance tax privileges. If well-off seniors must forgo part of their Social Security and Medicare benefits, so too must well-off farmers, veterans, federal pensioners, and corporations forgo some share of their own federal benefits. Every group, must bear part of the burden, but the contributions of the broad middle class, because of its size, must be greatest of all.

The political obstacles to entitlement reform are daunting, and cannot be overcome unless everyone sacrifices fairly and sees that sacrifice is necessary and will make a significant difference. Somehow, we must recapture the "we're all in it together" spirit Americans shared during World War II. Al-

though the challenge is very different, the threat to our national future is just as real.

Ask for progressive sacrifice. Progressivity—meaning that the more you get, the more you give—should be a bedrock principle of our entitlement system no less than of our tax system. But our current system of federal entitlements is far from FDR's original vision of a floor of protection against destitution. Three quarters of federal entitlement dollars flow through programs that do not take financial need into account in determining eligibility, a fact which results in huge windfalls for middle- and upper-income Americans. As we have seen, $270 billion, or 43 percent, of federal entitlement outlays in 1991 went to households with incomes above the national median; back-door tax benefits, like the home mortgage interest deduction and the tax exclusion for employer-paid health care, brought the 1991 total to $372 billion. In the five years since then, as I have indicated earlier, I estimate that this dollar total has grown by at least one third—to about $500 billion.

Entitlement reform must honor our commitment to protect the elderly poor and indeed should strengthen that protection. But the only way to do this is to trim the indiscriminate largesse government now hands out to the relatively well off. A strong safety net for the poor, without unsustainable deficits or tax hikes, means less for those with substantial incomes of their own.

This is why a comprehensive "affluence test" is essential to any reform plan. The test I propose would affect no household with an income beneath $40,000 (roughly $5,000 above the U.S. median in 1996)—but it would reduce benefits to higher-income households on a steeply progressive basis. Some of the savings from this (and other) entitlement reforms I propose would be dedicated to increasing benefits for the elderly poor under SSI, the cash assistance program for needy retirees.

Recognize the realities of an aging society. Controlling costs is not enough. Reform must also restructure entitlement programs to meet the needs of an older society and economy. When the age wave hits full force just ten to fifteen years from now, practically every public cost associated with retirement will start rising much faster than such costs are rising today. Long before then, we must rethink outdated expectations that have become unaffordable in an era of slow labor-force growth and increasing health and life expectancy. Instead of looking forward to ever earlier retirement, with ever less financial preparation, we must develop a more responsible (and possibly more rewarding) ideal: the later retirement, the fuller savings account, the better use of experience and maturity in the workplace.

Current entitlement policies encourage seniors to spend the last third of their adult lives in unproductive leisure at public expense. Retirement ages under Social Security must be raised. Instead of trying to prove themselves "model employers," federal agencies, which now allow employees to retire at fifty-five with an unreduced pension that is indexed for life, should demonstrate their civic leadership by trimming this generosity.* At the same time, we ought to get rid of policies, such as the Social Security earnings test, that deter older Americans from working. A future of unremitting demographic pressure demands such reforms and the behavioral changes that will result.

Respect the principle of generational equity. Today's entitlement system is based on a huge generational injustice. Current beneficiaries are receiving benefit paybacks far in excess of their own and their employers' contributions. Most Baby Boomers, on the other hand, will suffer large losses—even in

---

* On the lavish generosity of federal pensions, see Neil Howe and Richard Jackson, *The Facts About Federal Pensions* (The Concord Coalition, 1995).

Even without major new medical breakthroughs, rising life spans will lengthen the years spent in retirement.

Years of life expectancy at age 65

21.0 "High-Cost" Projection

19.1 Official "Intermediate" Projection

17.2

12.6

1935   1995   2040

SOURCE: Social Security Administration (1995)

the unlikely event that still younger generations agree to the unthinkable tax hikes needed to pay the benefits Boomers are promised. This inequity is fiscally—and morally—unsustainable. The days when we could finance entitlement windfalls for ourselves by shifting the costs to a more numerous and affluent rising generation are over. To balance the sacrifices we ask of *tomorrow's* entitlement beneficiaries, those Americans who are older and able must contribute their fair share *today*.

Phase in reforms gradually. Reforms must be phased in gradually to avoid wrenching adjustments in individual incomes and expectations—and to minimize the risk to the economy of suddenly reduced consumer spending. But gradualism cannot become another excuse for delay. Reforms should be phased in over five years—not fifty. The one exception is my proposed hike in the Social Security retirement age. Since this reform will substantially affect the long-term plans of nonaffluent beneficiaries, who must be given adequate time to build up their private savings, a twenty-year phase-in would be appropriate.

Focus on long-term structural savings. The problem with today's entitlement system is first, last, and always that we are *spending too much*. Ad hoc fixes—raising taxes a bit this year, trimming COLAs a bit the next—will never achieve long-term cost containment. Only permanent, *structural* adjustments will control entitlement costs long term.

We can achieve the greatest long-term savings through structural reforms that reduce retirement benefits and slow the growth in per capita health-care costs. The budget savings from such reforms will not only be permanent, but will compound as the population ages and the number of federal beneficiaries grows. Remember: The total number of elderly is expected to at least double over the next half century—while

those eighty-five or over, who consume over twice as much health care per capita as the young elderly, will triple or quadruple.

The affluence test I propose will save $33 billion annually in Social Security alone by the year 2000. But by 2020, that saving would grow to about $110 billion; by 2030, it would grow to about $215 billion. My proposed hike in the Social Security retirement age will save $22 billion annually by the year 2000, about $260 billion by 2020, and about $460 billion by 2030. These are huge savings—enough, together with full benefit taxation, to erase Social Security's cash deficit through the year 2030 and keep the system at or near cash balance thereafter.[1]

The economic benefits from such structural reforms are twofold. Permanent cuts in Social Security's (or Medicare's) promised benefits reduce both the program's projected cash deficit and its current unfunded liability. Reducing the first boosts national savings directly by cutting the federal deficit. Reducing the second boosts it indirectly by encouraging households to save more on their own.

Always remember the bottom line. That bottom line—as Fed Chairman Alan Greenspan testified before the Kerrey-Danforth Commission—is the consolidated budget deficit and its impact on national savings. The benefit lobbies prefer to talk about trust-fund surpluses and long-term actuarial balance. Within this trust-fund accounting framework, a mere 2.2 percentage point payroll tax increase, enacted tomorrow, would increase the Social Security surplus enough to balance the system for the next seventy-five years. But this framework ignores what really matters: what Treasury must borrow each year in private capital markets to finance the gap between total federal outlays and total federal revenues, including FICA. Since FICA is a tax and all taxes are fungible, any current Social Security surplus is spent to cover other

government expenditures as soon as it is collected. It cannot be spent again to cover the program's future cash shortfall.

The benefit lobbies also argue that cuts are only justified in those programs—mainly Medicare and Medicaid—that are currently growing faster than the economy. But this too is fiscal nonsense. The real problem is *total* federal expenditures. So long as federal health-benefit programs remain so resistant to cost control, we must try all the harder to economize wherever else we can. For purposes of public relations, it may be comforting to segregate entitlement programs into separate compartments. But borrowing for one purpose will bankrupt us just as surely as borrowing for another.

Let us now move from theory to practice. The following specific reform proposals, taken together, will balance our entitlement system for the long term in keeping with the principles I've outlined.

Subject all federal benefits to an affluence test. As I have indicated, this test would progressively reduce entitlement benefits to all households with incomes over $40,000, or more than $5,000 *above* the 1996 household median income.* Households with incomes under $40,000 would retain their full government benefits. Higher-income households would lose 10 percent of all benefits that raise their total income above $40,000, plus 10 percent for each additional $10,000 in income. Thus, a household with $50,000 in total income and $10,000 in federal benefits would lose 10 percent, or

---

* While this affluence test would affect only direct federal benefits, we must also reduce tax expenditures—implicit entitlements that the federal budget hands out by selectively exempting certain kinds of income from taxation and that are even more likely to go to the non-needy than are direct benefits. The consumption tax plan I propose below would eliminate numerous back-door entitlements, including corporate tax subsidies, the home mortgage interest deduction, and the unlimited tax exemption for employer-paid health care. See my book *Facing Up* for a fuller discussion.

$1,000, of its benefits; a household with the same $10,000 in benefits and $100,000 in income would lose 60 percent, or $6,000; a household with the same benefits and more than $120,000 in income would lose 85 percent, or $8,500—the maximum benefit withholding rate. (Exempting 15 percent of benefits from withholding insures that all current retirees will continue to enjoy a modest tax-free return on their personal Social Security FICA contributions.) The affluence test would be applied *annually*—protecting the elderly in the case of unexpected setbacks, such as a sudden loss of income. Needless to say, all income brackets would be indexed for inflation.

Since the test would leave in place all benefits to lower-income households, the floor of protection that Social Security and most other entitlements were originally intended to provide would not be affected. Since such a large share of entitlements now goes to middle- and upper-income Americans, the savings would be large and, as we have seen, would compound as the population ages and the number of beneficiaries grows. By the year 2000, the total *annual* entitlement savings under this affluence test would come to $70 billion—a sum that would surge to over $200 billion annually by 2020 and over $550 billion by 2040.[2] Finally, since the test would also be comprehensive, including not just Social Security and Medicare but everything from farm aid to federal pensions to veterans' benefits, this reform would not pit one special-interest constituency against another.

An affluence test has clear advantages over other approaches to across-the-board entitlement savings. We might, for instance, try to scale back subsidies for the relatively well off by rewriting the benefit formulas and eligibility criteria of Social Security and every other entitlement program. But this process would have to snake through dozens of congressional committees, risking ambush at every turn by lobbies bent on ensuring that their constituencies are not singled out for sac-

rifice. Alternatively, we could progressively reduce cost-of-living adjustments for beneficiaries with larger-than-average benefits. Until I developed the affluence test idea, I supported just such a reform. Benefit-related COLA cuts, however, cannot distinguish between a retired civil servant with two pensions and a small Social Security benefit and a retired widow living alone who subsists entirely on a bigger-than-average Social Security check. The affluence test avoids this problem because it considers *total* household income, not merely federal benefits, and thus cannot inadvertently hurt households beneath the national median. As for higher-earning households, the progressive sacrifices it calls for will always be based on beneficiaries' true and complete financial circumstances in any given year.

Much evidence now suggests that the Consumer Price Index overstates the actual rate of inflation by as much as 1 to 2 percent. If this is indeed the case—as numerous experts, including a 1995 blue-ribbon congressional commission headed by Michael Boskin, former Chairman of the Council of Economic Advisers, believe—we should fix it. It is unfair to overcompensate beneficiaries according to overstated inflation figures—especially when the wages of so many workers, whose taxes support those beneficiaries, lag far behind inflation. Even a small technical adjustment in this respect could yield significant savings. After all, COLAs on Social Security and other entitlements will add roughly $200 billion to cumulative federal expenditures over the next five years. A technical COLA correction is therefore important. A number of mainstream policy makers believe that a reduction of the annual COLA by one half of 1 percent can now be justified. If this were implemented now, it would result in savings of about 4 percent of projected Social Security outlays by 2020. While this is meaningful, we must bear in mind that future benefits will need to be reduced by 25 to 35 percent to stay within the trust funds cash revenues. But apart from such a

correction, I have come to believe that an affluence test is the fairest way to achieve large across-the-board savings.

Since this affluence test was first proposed in my book *Facing Up*—then adopted by The Concord Coalition—it has attracted considerable interest from Democrats as well as Republicans. But it has also been criticized by those who for various reasons oppose entitlement reform. Some critics have said that an affluence test would constitute a tax on savings and would thus discourage household thrift. But to argue that an affluence test is a major deterrent to savings presupposes that people will voluntarily pass up the chance to accumulate *personal* wealth today, during their working years, in order to collect more generous federal benefits during their retirement years, several decades later. This strains credibility. More important, this criticism ignores the larger issue—which is to increase national savings. Even if some households do save less because of the affluence test, any small decline in private savings will be dwarfed by the decline in benefit outlays—which in turn would translate *dollar for dollar* into smaller deficits and higher net national savings.

Other critics paradoxically claim that subjecting Social Security and other universal social insurance programs to an affluence test will destroy the safety net. This theory presupposes that upper-income households must be bribed with generous benefits in order to ensure their political support for programs that also benefit the needy. As the critics put it, "Programs for the poor are poor programs." It is curious that many of those who make this case against affluence testing favor both progressive taxation of Social Security benefits and a more progressive Social Security benefit formula. Conceptually, there is little difference between benefit taxation and an affluence test—except that in the first case government hands out windfalls and then taxes them away while in the second it dispenses with the revolving door. But more important, these critics misjudge the character of the American

Result of three reforms: Social Security would have a modest surplus through the year 2030.

Annual operating balance of the Social Security (Old-Age, Survivors, and Disability Insurance) trust funds: official "intermediate" projection

Projected surplus in 2030 after three reforms:

$8 billion

Projected current-law deficit in 2030:

$766 billion

REFORM ONE
Raise Social Security retirement age

Savings:
$461 billion

REFORM TWO
Apply affluence test

Savings:
$216 billion

REFORM THREE
Make more benefits taxable

Savings:
$97 billion

SOURCE: Social Security Administration (1995) and author's calculations

Result of three reforms: Social Security would be sustainable far into the twenty-first century.

Annual operating balance of the Social Security (Old-Age, Survivors, and Disability Insurance) trust funds, in billions of dollars: official "intermediate" projection

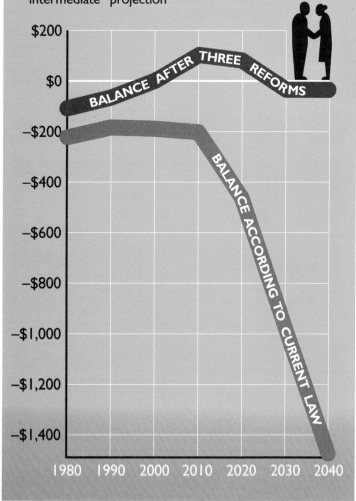

SOURCE: Social Security Administration (1995) and author's calculations

people and their willingness to support the needy. Of all major proposals to reform entitlements, affluence testing receives the greatest public support. According to a recent Concord Coalition opinion poll, 67 percent of those asked support reductions in Social Security benefits to higher-income households; 77 percent would support such reductions in Medicare benefits. Even majorities of older and affluent households support an affluence test.[3]

Although the "universalist" defense of the entitlements status quo is most often heard from liberals, conservatives sometimes reach the same conclusion by a different route. Many on the right *oppose* means-testing Social Security and Medicare for much the same reason that they *advocate* cutting welfare: They fear that a means test would reward spendthrifts who won't save just as welfare (in their view) rewards freeloaders who won't work. But when it comes to young families, their solution is to slash benefits for everyone. When it comes to seniors, their solution is to defend benefits for everyone. Perversely, the conservative horror of undeserved welfare inclines them to put everyone on the dole.

I certainly acknowledge that some well-to-do seniors will feel that an affluence test penalizes them because they were thrifty during their working years—and will resent the fact that their less thrifty peers are getting more generous benefits. But most of the elderly poor are not poor because they were profligate. They are poor because they worked most of their lives in low-paying jobs. In any case, we are dealing with a condition, not a theory: We must find some way of controlling the unsustainable growth in entitlement benefits, and an affluence test is, in my opinion, the best and most practical option.

Raise the eligibility age for benefits. Most Americans may not be aware of it, but Congress has already raised the Social Security full-benefit retirement age from sixty-five to sixty-seven, to be phased in between 2000 and 2027. This is a step

in the right direction but far too small and slow. The Social Security full-benefit retirement age should be raised by three months a year until a new eligibility age of seventy is reached in 2015. This would leave Boomers plenty of time to plan ahead. In my opinion, early retirement should still be allowed at age sixty-two, but the benefits extended to early retirees should be reduced commensurately. When these reforms are entirely phased in, workers retiring at age seventy will still enjoy more years of full benefits than had originally been envisioned when Social Security was founded. As Social Security's full-benefit eligibility age rises to seventy, so should Medicare's. Americans aged sixty-five to sixty-nine could still participate in the program, but only by paying extra premiums.

Set limits on federal health-benefit spending. Health benefits must be restructured to control federal health-care costs. Currently, fee-for-service reimbursement is offered to all eligible comers with few cost disincentives, and the process is then surrounded by a thicket of ineffective regulatory controls. I propose instead that Medicare, Medicaid, and other federal health-benefit programs offer beneficiaries three choices:

- a fixed-dollar voucher to use toward the purchase of the health insurance of their choice or
- membership in an accredited managed-care program, such as an HMO or a preferred provider organization (PPO), that will then bill the government a fixed annual charge or
- the current fee-for-service system, but with much greater copayments and deductibles

Any reform that seeks to introduce market discipline into our system of federal health benefits must give beneficiaries real incentives to consider costs, which is why I require greater copayments and deductibles for those who choose the more expensive fee-for-service option. Congress's recent pro-

posal to overhaul Medicare was a small carrot and no stick. It would simply have given beneficiaries the option of enrolling in HMOs without penalizing those who remained in the fee-for-service system.

The measures I propose will shift the task of cost control away from regulators and back to patients and providers, where it belongs. My plan would also allow Congress to live within a health-benefits budget, just as the government of every other industrial country does. As for the senior lobby and its demand for a "free choice of doctor" guarantee, the elderly need to be reminded that a declining proportion of today's young workers—whose FICA taxes pay for much of Medicare—enjoys the full freedom of choice that was once common in American medicine. Indeed, most young workers are lucky if their employer pays for any health insurance at all. Why, then, should they subsidize "free choice" for their elders?

Another candidate for reform is the unlimited tax exemption for company-paid health-care insurance—an indirect entitlement that now costs the federal Treasury $92 billion a year.[4] This costly and regressive tax subsidy benefits relatively well paid Americans and offers nothing to the poor, unemployed, or uninsured. Moreover, because this exemption benefits most those who choose the most expensive and permissive insurance plans, it encourages people to spend more on health care than they otherwise would. Under the new consumed income tax system I propose below, employer-paid health insurance would automatically be counted and taxed as ordinary employee income. But we do not have to reinvent the tax system to reform this wasteful subsidy. Congress could simply cap the allowable exemption at the average cost of an insurance policy. At the same time, it should enact long overdue reforms of insurance regulations so that workers are guaranteed that health insurance is portable and not subject to exclusions for preexisting conditions.

Effective health-care reform requires national health-practice guidelines that establish what services government will or will not reimburse. Yet perversely, Congress now proposes to cut funds for the "health outcomes" research that will make such guidelines possible—research that promises to pay for itself many times over. Although these standards would not prohibit patients or providers from spending their own money for services above the guidelines, they would give everyone a much clearer idea of the cost effectiveness of various treatment options, something all experts agree we lack.

We must also reduce the huge costs of "defensive medicine" through malpractice reform and of "heroic" intervention where recovery is unlikely. As we have seen, Medicare spends nearly *30 percent* of its budget on patients in their last year of life—often when attempts to prolong life merely delay a hospitalized death. Few Americans want to end their days this way. According to a recent survey, 89 percent of us believe that living wills are a good idea. The problem is that only 9 percent of us actually have one. Until we launch a massive educational campaign about the importance of advance medical directives, make enforceable living wills widely available at low cost, and perhaps even provide modest financial incentives to maintain them, doctors will continue to perform costly and painful procedures for patients who do not (or would not) want them and who will die in a few days or weeks anyway.

Finally, we must face tough choices about the most explosive cost of senior dependency: long-term care for the frail elderly. Medicaid, the health-benefit program which is jointly administered by the states and the federal government, currently pays for about half of all U.S. nursing home bills. Though nominally a means-tested program for which only the elderly poor are eligible, the test is so riddled with loopholes that middle- and upper-income seniors easily qualify. Among Americans aged sixty-five and over, only 12 percent are below the official poverty line—and fewer than 7 percent

receive means-tested cash assistance under the SSI program. But over half of seniors get a Medicaid subsidy from the day they enter a nursing home.[5]

Two facts make this gentrification of Medicaid unaffordable. First, per capita nursing home spending on the frail elderly aged eighty-five and over is *over twenty times higher* than spending on the young elderly, aged sixty-five to sixty-nine. Second, the number of these frail elderly is expected to triple or quadruple as America ages. We have no choice but to close loopholes that allow seniors to qualify for Medicaid through subterfuge—for instance, by transferring assets to their children. The government—that is, the taxpayers—can no longer pay for long-term care for middle- and upper-income families who are able to save, insure, and pool resources on their own. These families must be encouraged to purchase private long-term care insurance—something Medicaid's de facto universal entitlement now gives them no incentive to do. Everyone agrees that it's bad policy for dependent children to become wards of the state without first demanding that parents live up to their responsibilities. But what about deadbeat kids? No doubt this suggestion will offend the senior lobby, which claims that federal subsidies give the elderly the "dignity of independence"—as if relying on your grown children rather than the public Treasury is ignoble dependence.

3. Extend Working Lives

Encouraging seniors to work longer—and making it easier for them to do so—obviously requires more than simply raising the eligibility age for full benefits under Social Security and Medicare. We must also abolish the current Social Security "earnings test," which withholds benefits from seniors who continue to work. This change, however, should be part of a package of reforms that includes an affluence test. Con-

gress, always ready to give but never to take away, recently passed a stand-alone liberalization of the earnings test that will provide an unearned windfall for higher-income seniors. Eliminating the earnings test would cost the Treasury $5 billion or so a year in extra Social Security payments to working retirees, but the benefit to the economy, as well as to the seniors themselves, of continuing productive activity will be far greater than this small cost.[6] Another relatively inexpensive reform with big potential payoffs is to make Medicare the "primary" health insurer for beneficiaries who continue to work, so that employers, who are now the primary payer, will be less reluctant to hire the elderly.

The maturity, wisdom, and experience of older adults should not be lost to the workplace. The issue is not simply combating age discrimination but unlocking a powerful human resource. Contrary to popular stereotype, recent studies show that productivity does not fall—and may even rise—among workers in their sixties and seventies.[7] An aging society should seek ways to tap this resource—part-time or full-time—in health care or child care or the dozens of other fields for which the elderly are well suited.

Some critics worry that if the economy employs more seniors, the young won't find jobs. This may have been a legitimate concern during the Great Depression, when unemployment averaged over 22 percent. Indeed, when Social Security was first founded, one of its explicit purposes was to get the old out of the labor force in order to make room for the young. But a growing economy does not pit workers against one another in a zero-sum competition for jobs. It creates new jobs. The Social Security Administration projects that the growth of the U.S. labor force will slow to near zero in the 2010s and 2020s as the Baby Boom retires. The real danger is not that there will be too many people looking for jobs in the next century but that there won't be enough.

Turbocharged senior benefits: Can they be funded by a slow-growth workforce?

Major federal benefits to seniors* (in real dollars) versus working-age population: official "intermediate" projection

Major Senior Benefits

Population Age 20–64

500

400

300

200

Index: 1990= 100

1990   2000   2010   2020   2030   2040

SOURCE: Social Security Administration (1994) and National Taxpayers Union Foundation (1994)
*Major senior benefits are Social Security, Medicare, and senior benefits under Medicaid.

I have been fortunate to find many opportunities for meaningful work well past the traditional retirement age. As I approached sixty, I founded a new company. Today, at age seventy, I am still working full-time and can't imagine quitting. Why should antiquated Social Security regulations discourage millions of others from doing the same?

Not everyone, of course, can continue to work. Richard Trumka, President of the United Mine Workers, warned the Kerrey-Danforth Commission on which we both served that later retirement is simply not a realistic option for worn-out laborers in physically demanding occupations. Such workers, however, are a small and shrinking share of the total labor force. Under my plan, they could still choose early retirement (though with reduced benefits) and would be protected by federal Disability Insurance and Workers' Compensation, not to mention the system of mandatory personal retirement accounts for future retirees that I shall propose below. I would also use a small part of the savings from raising the Social Security retirement age and implementing an affluence test to reduce eligibility ages and raise benefit levels for SSI, the means-tested floor of protection for the low-income elderly. In other words, we must take care to protect those seniors who are incapacitated and cannot continue on the job. But our overall national retirement policy should not be determined by the retiring miner at age sixty-two any more than by the retiring police officer at fifty-two or the retiring athlete at forty-two.

4. Establish a System of Mandatory Pensions or Personal Retirement Accounts

Balancing the budget—or even running a modest surplus—is not enough to meet the required savings and productivity goals. We must also raise the private savings rate. I have therefore concluded, reluctantly, that we should institute a

system of *mandatory, fully funded, personally owned, privately managed, and portable* pension accounts for future retirees. The system I envisage would initially supplement Social Security benefits—and in time would increasingly replace them, though Social Security would continue to provide a floor of protection for all Americans, subject to the affluence test described above.

So far, industrial countries have tried to accomplish both of these goals—protection of the poor and retirement saving—in a single universal pay-as-you-go program. These programs have typically done neither job well. As the recent World Bank Study, *Averting the Old Age Crisis*, explains, pay-as-you-go social insurance, in which retirement "savings" consists of nothing more than claims on future taxes, inevitably leads to high and rising tax rates and declining returns on lifetime contributions. Moreover, to the extent that it alleviates poverty, it is by sheer dint of the massive sums spent, not by effectively targeting benefits to those who need them. Above some floor of protection, retirement saving is best accomplished through—well, savings. Ideally, only the safety net should be financed with tax dollars.

Why mandatory? In 1993, C. Fred Bergsten, Director of the Competitiveness Policy Council, a publicly financed bipartisan group, asked me to chair a committee on capital formation. An impressive collection of the nation's leading economists joined me in this effort. I had expected to hear that certain tax favors for savings—IRAs, for example—could significantly increase *net* savings. I quickly learned otherwise. The net savings effect of many of these conventional incentives has been marginal because people simply shifted much of the money deposited in IRAs out of other investments in order to enjoy the tax advantage without significantly increasing their overall savings.

When I asked the committee how to increase *net* savings

significantly, one important area of agreement emerged: mandatory pensions or retirement accounts covering the entire workforce, not just those workers most likely to save anyway. In addition to boosting private savings, such plans—by making tomorrow's retirees more self-sufficient—could allow us to reduce future Social Security benefits gradually, thus reducing public dissavings as well.

I am fully aware of the libertarian argument that all decisions about savings should be left up to individuals. After the great health reform debate of 1994–95, it has also become clear that any proposal involving mandates will face significant political obstacles, especially the opposition of small employers worried about labor costs. The melancholy truth, however, is that millions of Americans whose earnings permit them to save choose not to. Therefore, to prevent large numbers of retirees from becoming free riders on the public safety net, a national pension plan must be mandatory.

Why fully funded? First, because a funded retirement system will add to America's capital stock and thus help raise productivity and national income. A pay-as-you-go system will not. Second, because a funded system prevents one generation from burdening the next: Above a minimum safety net, retirement benefits will be determined *solely* by the resources that have been accumulated personally by individuals through some combination of employer contributions and their own savings. Finally, because a funded system will allow workers to earn much higher rates of return on their contributions. Many critics, myself included, have argued that windfall paybacks to today's Social Security beneficiaries are a good argument for reform: Why not reduce these windfalls while still leaving the beneficiaries a decent rate of return? So far, this argument has fallen on deaf ears. Ironically, as we near the end of the Social Security chain letter, the opposite

argument may turn out to be more persuasive: Why not reform a system that cannot possibly offer younger participants
the same long-term rate of return as assets invested in the real
economy?

Lest I be misunderstood, let me spell out a crucial distinction. *The fundamental issue is not public versus private but
unfunded versus funded.* What I am proposing is to *fund*
Social Security, not to *privatize* it. Workers' savings accounts
would be personally owned and invested in private capital
markets. But contributions would be mandatory, and account balances would be subject to use restrictions. When lib-
ertarians talk about privatization, they usually mean handing
FICA taxes back to workers to save or not as they please. My
plan would not abolish Social Security. It would refashion it
as a compulsory savings system backed up by an ironclad
guarantee of protection against poverty in old age.

Why personally owned? When Social Security was founded
in 1935, it was officially projected to cost 6 percent of payroll
in 1995 and every year thereafter. Today Social Security costs
11.5 percent of payroll and is projected to cost between 17
and 22 percent of payroll by 2040. But the prospect of ever-
rising tax rates—and dwindling paybacks on FICA contributions—is not the only intergenerational injustice resulting
from the Social Security chain letter. To the extent that
promised pay-as-you-go benefits are unaffordable, future
Congresses will have to renege on them. In contrast, personally owned retirement savings, invested in the real economy,
cannot be taken away. Ironically, Social Security was originally set up because people trusted the government more than
they trusted financial markets. Today's young Americans feel
just the opposite. They understand that they will have to continue paying FICA taxes to support current retirees. But when
it comes to their own retirement, the great majority would
prefer an account with real assets in their own name.

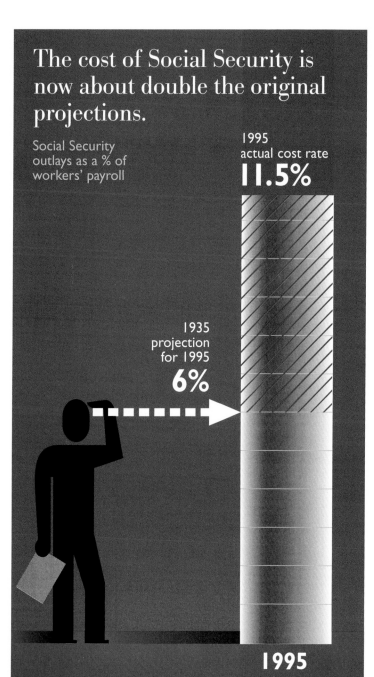

The cost of Social Security is now about double the original projections.

Social Security outlays as a % of workers' payroll

1995 actual cost rate
11.5%

1935 projection for 1995
6%

1995

SOURCE: Social Security Administration (1995)

Why privately managed? Any system of mandatory savings must be subject to strict public regulation to maintain fiduciary standards. But to the extent possible, investment accounts should be privately managed to maximize returns. The evidence shows that publicly managed systems—which are often required by law to invest in government securities or government-designated industries—earn far less than privately managed systems. Still, in any plan, the federal government will have to serve as "default fiduciary" for those workers who refuse or are unable to deal with a certified private investment fund. These workers' savings would be invested according to a formula that is relatively low risk (it would include both Treasury bonds and stock market indexes), but which would still give them a rate of return comparable to that of most workers with "sophisticated" financial advice.*

Why portable? "Lifetime employment" with one company has become rare in the new and fluid global economy, characterized by intense competition, rapid innovation, and relentless technological change. In fact, seven or eight major job changes in a lifetime are now the norm. As a result, many workers lack enough years of service with one company to qualify for a traditional defined benefit pension—or if they do qualify, the benefit is small. The plan I propose would therefore vest all contributions immediately, which would allow workers to take their pension accounts with them as they get "downsized" or move from job to job.

For these accounts to provide adequate retirement income, workers, in some combination with employers, will have to

---

* We have not repealed sustained bear markets. For example, between the summer of 1966 and 1982, there was virtually no gain at all in the Dow-Jones. Thus, a significant share of all such portfolios should be in near risk-free bonds.

make substantial contributions—perhaps as much as 5 percent of pay. Assuming (conservatively) that the real return on pension accounts averages 4.5 percent per year, this contribution would offer most workers an annual retirement benefit considerably greater than Social Security as a percentage of preretirement income.* And this is just the mandatory minimum. Workers could choose to make additional voluntary contributions, and employers who currently provide pensions could divert contributions to these accounts as well. The primary goal is to finance retirement and survivors' benefits—though in time it might also pay for long-term care.

Although mandatory savings contributions would initially be in addition to the current FICA payroll tax and would thus decrease the consumable portion of each paycheck, the new system would be linked to the cost-saving reforms (affluence testing and a higher Social Security retirement age) proposed above. At a minimum, these reforms guarantee that FICA tax rates will never rise above today's level. In the future, the reforms could be made more stringent, allowing us to cut FICA taxes well *beneath* today's level. Eventually, workers would be paying no more (and probably substantially less) in combined FICA and savings contributions under my plan than they are now paying in FICA taxes alone. The difference is that they will be accumulating real savings of their own which future Congresses cannot take away.

* Over the past two hundred years, the real rate of return on U.S. business equity (i.e., stocks) has averaged just over 6.5 percent per year. The real rate of return on risk-free debt (i.e., Treasury bonds) has averaged just over 3 percent per year. My assumption is thus based on very long-term historical averages with a conservative mix of equity and debt. Some eminent economists, including Martin Feldstein, believe the return would be higher. Feldstein argues that a large increase in private savings in the form of corporate equity would generate large additions to federal, state, and local revenues via corporate income and property taxes. Any such additional revenue represents a net gain to society and could be used to offset other taxes. Alternatively, it could be cycled back into Social Security—which would allow us to get by with more modest benefit cuts than those I proposed.

My plan would also require that any current-year Social Security cash surplus be transferred to workers' personal accounts. And if future Social Security outlays decline as a percentage of payroll, the share of FICA revenues credited to workers' accounts would grow, thus giving them a direct stake in reforms that limit the cost of Social Security.

Let me repeat: I propose a two-tiered system in which all retirees will continue to receive Social Security. If the public so chooses, however, my reform could be taken a step further. As private retirement accounts increase, the affluence test can gradually be made stricter, until the current universal Social Security system becomes a much less costly floor of protection that only pays benefits to the truly needy.

At the national level, my plan would generate substantial increases in net savings—and thus contribute to higher productivity and living standards. These additional savings are essential to a fully funded Social Security system. Productivity will not rise unless we save more during the transition. Some "reformers" believe that merely by investing some or all of workers' current FICA contributions in private capital markets everyone will be better off in the long run.* Yes they know that Treasury will have to borrow to make up for the missing revenue. But apparently they believe that Treasury (or each worker's account) will earn greater returns (with no greater risks) on the stock assets than would be lost on the additional debt liabilities.

Many of these reforms would have government invest some or all of current Social Security trust-fund surpluses in the stock market. This plan does have one potential benefit.

---

* While additional equity purchases may increase Social Security returns, the rates of return on private pensions and for other equity holders would fall, since they would, in effect, be swapping the additional treasury bonds that would otherwise have gone into the trust fund. What matters in the long run is the *aggregate* return to the *economy*. To increase these aggregate returns, we must increase savings; as a practical matter, this must include reduced benefits.

It may force Congress and the President to balance the budget without counting these surpluses.

But any plan that intends to cash in on the spread between stocks and bonds is dicey. If the federal government starts buying stocks and selling fixed-interest debt on a large scale, the yield on bonds will rise and the yield on stocks will fall—narrowing the favorable spread that the plan depends on. Moreover, the very fact that government is betting on the stock market to defray the cost of future benefit payments will raise the risk (and hence the interest cost) of government debt. No major country engages in this sort of arbitrage—not just because of the offsetting (economic) effect on interest rates, but also because of the corrosive (political) effect on the "full faith and credit" of government itself.* On the other hand, if some or all FICA taxes are put into individual worker accounts, the extra interest payable to new government debt holders will largely cancel out the (risk-adjusted) return to account holders. In the long run, this revolving door is just as unlikely to leave society better off.

By increasing national saving, my plan would do more than help the economy. It would also increase individual retirement incomes and guarantee retirement security. For middle- and upper-income workers subject upon retirement to the affluence test, my proposed pension accounts would at least make up for reduced government retirement benefits—and probably much more. For lower-income retirees, those least likely to save (either on their own or through employer pensions), these accounts would vastly reduce the odds of destitute retirement from what the odds are under our current system. If retirees' earnings fall beneath the affluence test

---

* If it did make sense for the government to go into the arbitrage business, one wonders why it should stop with Social Security. Why doesn't it always make sense for the Treasury to borrow trillions of dollars, invest the funds in the stock market, make a bundle of money, then refund the profits to taxpayers? To ask the question is to answer it.

threshold, the income from their pension accounts will add to their *full* government benefits.

To ease the burden of payroll contributions on low-income workers—and to ensure that they accumulate adequate retirement income—I would also provide for savings subsidies. For workers earning up to $10,000 a year, the government would match personal contributions 1.5 to 1. Perhaps one third of this match could be made a refundable tax credit so that at low-income levels the effective individual contribution rate would be no more than 2.5 percent of pay. For those with incomes above $10,000, the subsidy would be phased out so that it falls to zero for households earning the median income (about $35,000 in 1996). Yes, even a 2.5 percent payroll contribution could be a burden for low-income families. But it's worth noting that because of the Earned Income Tax Credit, the existing FICA tax burden on many of the working poor is now entirely borne by the federal government.

The idea behind these subsidies is akin to preventative medicine: Let's do everything we can to ensure that workers with low lifetime incomes don't find themselves both old and poor. But like any doctor, we must also provide for cases where prevention doesn't work. My plan would guarantee all Americans aged sixty-two and over a means-tested floor of protection equal to 120 percent of the poverty line. Today, the SSI program guarantees a floor of income protection for the elderly equal to just 70 percent of the poverty line for single beneficiaries and 90 percent for couples. Moreover, eligibility for SSI starts at sixty-five. My plan would thus provide substantially more generous poverty protection than current law. An expansion of the safety net has long been advocated by the Urban Institute and other liberal think tanks. But until we're willing to make some tough choices about entitlements (like increasing the retirement age and affluence-testing Social Security, Medicare, and other federal benefits), we can't afford it.

And what about the middle class? Won't a 5 percent contribution—even if shared by the employer—be a real sacrifice for a family struggling to get by on $35,000 a year? Of course it will. But let's also bear in mind that a mandatory savings contribution is not a tax. Families will be contributing to their own savings accounts, and these accounts will accumulate tax free (just like a 401[k] plan). True, there would be restrictions on how families could use their pension funds. But above the amount needed to fund a minimum annual retirement benefit, retirees would be permitted to do what they want with their account balances, including passing them on to their heirs, something that is impossible with Social Security. Many families will welcome the opportunity to do something—save for their own and their children's future—that the vast majority confess they should be doing anyway.

There is also more room for sacrifice than some politicians, determined to exploit middle-class anxieties, would have us believe. Middle-class Americans still have higher incomes (and consume a much larger share of their incomes and pay far less of their incomes in taxes) than their counterparts in Europe and Japan. Most Americans are not worse off than they were twenty years ago—much less thirty or fifty. The problem is that wages have stopped growing, shattering the expectation of a rising standard of living. For living standards to grow again, we must save more—which is precisely what my mandatory pension proposal is all about. Unfortunately, there is no way to save more without also consuming less, at least temporarily, which is simply another way of saying that there is no solution that does not require sacrifice.

Every American—whether a CEO or his or her secretary—has a stake in the productivity gains that more savings will bring, since it is only these productivity gains that can ultimately generate both higher wages and higher profits. Any reform plan that boosts national savings will thus benefit workers. The plan I propose, however, would doubly benefit

them, for not only will they share in productivity gains through higher wages but they will also share in them through the profits they earn as owners of corporate capital.

In the early 1970s, some visionaries talked about how the rapid growth in pensions would soon lead to a new kind of capitalism—a "pension fund" capitalism in which workers, in effect, would own the tools of production. Maybe it's time to resurrect that vision.

Dismissed until recently as too radical, alternative plans to fund Social Security have multiplied over the past year. As I have noted, major proposals are under development at half a dozen U.S. think tanks—left, right, and center. To one extent or another, a majority of the administration's official Social Security Advisory Council favors supplementing or replacing today's pay-as-you-go system with a system of funded and personally owned defined contribution accounts.*

My plan has elements in common with many of these proposals, but it differs from most in that it *fully acknowledges and fully pays for the transition cost to a funded Social Security system.* Some proposals under consideration also acknowledge and propose to pay for this cost, but my plan differs from these in that it *pays for the transition without adding to the national debt and without new general purpose tax increases.*

The challenge is that a single generation must somehow pay for two retirements, its own and that of its parents. Some proposals, such as the plan floated by Steve Forbes during his run for the Republican presidential nomination, would retain benefits for current retirees but permit younger workers to shift a part of their FICA taxes into personal retirement accounts. What these plans add to private savings will likely be canceled out dollar for dollar by a larger federal deficit.

---

* As I've also noted, Senators Bob Kerrey and Alan Simpson have proposed legislation to set up a (modest) system of funded accounts as part of a comprehensive program of Social Security reform that includes increased retirement ages and COLA reductions.

Other proposals would issue trillions of dollars of Treasury obligations directly to Social Security beneficiaries in the amount of their accrued benefit claims. This too is likely to be a zero-sum game that leaves tomorrow's workers little or no better off than if the system had never been reformed in the first place.* A few proposals, like that of the Social Security Advisory Council, are more honest. But they would resort to large general purpose tax increases to pay for the transition—an approach that besides being politically problematic will hopelessly muddy the rationale for sacrifice and leave the public wondering why it is being asked to give something up.

My plan would pay for transition costs within the Social Security system itself by asking current beneficiaries to forgo some benefits and by asking current workers to save more. This will not be painless. The "magic" of compounded stock market returns cannot alone solve our problem. As I have said, to save more, we must consume less, at least temporarily. This "transition cost"—a temporary reduction in consumption—is the price of escaping the generational chain letter we have so far depended upon. It will hurt, but given the alternative, the temporary pain is well worth it.

Among others, the National Thrift Plan Project, sponsored by the Center for Public Policy and Contemporary Issues and the National Taxpayers Union Foundation, is beginning to approach the challenge along similar lines.[8] The transition

---

* However the accounts are shuffled, the bottom line is the same. To finance current-law benefits (or to pay off recognition bonds as they come due), Treasury will have to borrow from private capital markets. In effect, government will be subtracting from private savings with one hand what it has just added to it with the other. The only difference is that issuing recognition bonds to Social Security participants *formalizes* the system's implicit unfunded liability, thus putting future Social Security costs (truly and not just rhetorically) beyond the control of Congress. If recognition bonds were issued to cover Social Security's entire existing unfunded liability, the present value of the new formal debt would initially equal $8 trillion. Each year this debt is not paid off, the total would grow by about $600 billion.

cost to a funded Social Security system is enormous—and the hazards are many. Careful economic modeling of the transition, like that the National Thrift Plan team is undertaking, is the essential first step, for we cannot, obviously, succumb to the allure of private accounts without thinking through the transition problem in detail.

5. Shift Our Tax Base from Income to Consumption

Thomas Hobbes once wrote: "It is fairer to tax people on what they extract from the economy as roughly measured by their consumption than to tax them on what they produce for the economy, as roughly measured by their income." To be sure, Hobbes was no bleeding heart. But he was one of the first philosophers to reflect systematically on questions of social happiness—and the first of many economists to advocate using consumption rather than income as the tax base. In an aging society like ours in which we must encourage savings, it is more important than ever that we heed Hobbes's argument. I therefore propose that only "consumed income"— that is, income minus all forms of savings—be taxed. Exempting savings from taxation will narrow the tax base. But this proposal would also widen the tax base by taxing various forms of government-subsidized consumption—from Social Security to the insurance value of Medicare to employer-paid health care—which today are partially or fully exempt from income taxes. The average tax rate thus need not be any higher than it is today.

Consumption taxes are widely criticized as regressive. This is, however, an unfair generalization, for a consumption tax can be designed to be as progressive as our current income tax. One way to accomplish this is the consumed-income tax plan introduced by Senators Sam Nunn and Pete Domenici, in which progressive tax rates are levied each year on whatever income is left after taxpayers deduct what they have

saved and add in what they have borrowed. Borrowing is added to prevent people from gaming the system. If we didn't take borrowing into account, a taxpayer could take out a loan, turn around and deposit the money in an IRA and declare a deduction on his or her 1040. Needless to say, this transaction adds nothing to net savings.

Under the Nunn-Domenici plan, the more one consumes, the higher one's tax rate. The Congressional Budget Office has also concluded that, for nearly all taxpayers, a "saving-exempt income tax" system can easily be made as progressive as our current straight income tax system at tax rates close to today's.[9] Yes, to ensure that the super rich (who generally save the vast bulk of their income) pay their fair share, we might need to impose very high tax rates on their consumption—or even an extra income surtax. But why not? There is no reason that America's most affluent shouldn't pay much more for their consumption of luxuries if middle-income Americans are being asked to pay somewhat more for the consumption of necessities.

Although the basic concept is straightforward, most experts agree that many knotty transitional issues must be worked out before a consumed-income tax can be implemented. How exactly will "savings" be defined? Will only "new" savings be deductible, or will "old" savings be as well? If these issues prove insurmountable, my fall-back proposal is for a national sales tax with two or three modifications to make it as progressive as our current tax system. One would be an income surtax on the wealthy (those today in the top income tax bracket) to make sure they bear their fair burden. Another would be a refundable tax credit for families beneath the national median income. Yet another possible modification (used in many states, though it does narrow the tax base) would be to exempt certain basic household expenditures (food, for example) that account for a large share of the consumption of lower income households.

Progressivity is an important issue, but one that must be kept in perspective. Most economists agree that tax code changes have contributed relatively little to changes in the income equality of American families from one decade to the next. Structural changes in the economy are far more important. To the extent tax codes do make a difference, critics often overestimate the regressivity of a consumption tax. Although a person's income can vary widely from his or her consumption in any given year, there is much less variation over the length of an entire lifetime—since most people eventually consume most of what they save (for instance, in retirement). Thus, whatever revenue a consumption tax system forgoes this year by favoring individuals who saves more, it is likely to get back in a later year.

In any event, we must not forget the bottom line. Without higher savings, we cannot expect the real income of the typical American household to grow again—and without such growth, the polarization of incomes will continue to widen. In the end, the zero-sum politics of economic stagnation will overwhelm whatever weak contribution to economic equality we can expect from our current income tax system.

We are currently bombarded with a variety of tax reform proposals—from sales taxes to flat taxes. Some want to get rid of the IRS. Some want tax returns that can be filled out on a postcard, and so on. Who doesn't want simplicity? And who likes the impositions of the IRS on our privacy and freedom? But I would suggest a more important and overarching criterion for evaluating proposals for tax reform: *Which is most likely to increase net national savings?*

6. Mount a Massive "Savings Crusade" to Promote Thrift

I do not believe that America's denial syndrome results from some incurable moral pathology. What we suffer from is a

simple (if persistent) case of what my friend Dan Yankelovich calls "cognitive denial"—the failure to distinguish between reality and wishful thinking. Can the right kind of education and exhortation overcome our denial syndrome?

In the 1950s, Japan successfully rallied behind a national campaign to promote thrift. Before then, the Japanese were poor savers. Or consider Singapore, whose Central Provident Fund has furnished much of the investment capital that fuels Singapore's legendary economic growth—not to mention the savings that has enabled nine out of ten worker households to own their homes. Or consider Chile and Australia, which, as we have seen, have also established national pension systems based on the principles of full funding and portability. In all of these cases, public education was crucial to secure public support. Even in Chile's dictatorship the Minister of Labor and Social Welfare went on national television, often weekly, to explain why the mandatory pension plan was good for Chileans.

In a society like our own, where grassroots consensus is so important to governance, public discussion and debate are all the more important. The problem is that for at least three decades, leaders have been telling us that consumption, not savings, is the key to prosperity, a campaign that has worked all too well. Now it's time for a different kind of campaign— one in which not only our political leaders but also our businesses, our universities, and our public-policy institutions persuade Americans to adapt to the realities of our aging society.

What we need most of all is a moral vision, a "Middle-Class Bill of Responsibilities"—not a gaggle of leaders falling over one another in their rush to propose a new "Middle-Class Bill of Rights" or the middle-class mantra "We are not part of the problem, and we need not be part of the solution." We must now ask: What can we fairly expect individuals and families to do for themselves, and what should federal, state,

or local governments continue to do for them? To what extent can we count on families to provide for their elders? Today senior entitlements free retirees from an embarrassing dependence on their own children, but is it right for these retirees to depend on everybody else's children, regardless of their own and their families' means? Finally, what are our obligations as a nation to our collective progeny?

At first glance, the manual for Germany's social security system looks like our own: page after page describing the benefits if you retire, are widowed, or lose your job. The most obvious difference is the generous benefits to German children. But there is a more striking contrast. For each benefit, alongside a box describing "your rights," is a box describing "your duties." Citizens are thus reminded that society must balance the payer against the payee, the future against the present—a small step toward what the Europeans have come to call a sense of "generational solidarity."

Americans once understood this. Throughout our history, we have debated the two central questions of political life: Who benefits? Who pays? Farmers against bankers, consumers against the trusts, unions against corporations, New Dealers against Liberty Leaguers—in all of these struggles, no one questioned that the issue of costs would eventually have to be settled, one way or the other, *among the living,* not passed on to future generations. But in recent years, there has been an unspoken truce between "supply-siders," opposed to any tax increase, and "liberals," opposed to any cut in domestic spending. More often than not, both have gotten what they wanted, at the expense of a larger national debt.

Why can't the President call for a different kind of White House Conference on Aging from the one held last year—not one that panders to the senior lobby but one that encourages serious dialogue between old and young? And why can't the President call for a global summit in which the leading economies focus on reducing their massive unfunded liabili-

ties while developing economies, whose populations are younger, concentrate on avoiding the mistakes the industrial countries have made in providing for old-age security? We call such summits to talk about tariffs and exchange rates. Why not call one to talk about the enormous global economic challenge of unsustainable, unfunded liabilities? When I spoke with Margaret Thatcher about this challenge at a New York luncheon in early 1996, she agreed that unfunded benefit liabilities are the transcendent fiscal problem of the Big Seven countries. In fact, she told me that she had tried repeatedly to put this subject on their summit agenda, but without success. The political fall out, she said, was just too toxic. It's time to try again.

Corporations also need to join in the savings crusade by using their personnel and accounting departments to help educate workers on the basics of savings—how much to save to achieve a given retirement income, the power of compound interest, how to invest to maximize returns or minimize risk. They can also make it easier for their employees to save— through automatic salary deductions, 401(k) plans, stock purchase plans, and dividend reinvestment plans.

The Wyatt Company, an employee benefits consulting firm, reports that workers who use company educational materials are 20 percent more likely to participate in employer-sponsored retirement savings plans than those who do not. However, companies need to be careful that their educational efforts don't backfire. Retirement planning, of course, is a standard financial service offered by most brokerage firms. As part of this service, clients are often asked to fill out questionnaires detailing what level of income they hope to enjoy in retirement and what their current sources of retirement savings are, including Social Security and employer pensions. The firms then compute the client's "savings gap." Until they learned better, many firms reported this gap as a dollar total. Their thinking was that the typically huge figure would moti-

vate their clients to save and invest more. But this approach often had just the opposite effect: Many clients concluded that the goal was impossible to meet and so did nothing. Most brokerage firms now avoid reporting dollar totals and instead refer to savings goals in terms of dollar or percentage increments.

Bringing our *youth* into the savings crusade is essential. The young, alas, are the real silent majority. The demographer Samuel Preston once remarked that politicians would behave a lot differently if their constituents lived their lives backwards—that is, if they had to look forward to the burdens imposed upon youth as their own future. I hope that the young people who have read this book now see that it is, after all, *their* future we have been talking about.

When I speak at college commencements, I suggest that young people embark on dual careers—a personal career and a part-time career as citizens. As citizen lobbyists on behalf of the future, they must learn about the debts *they are being asked to assume,* the unfunded liabilities *they must defray,* and the unsustainable tax hikes that promise to wreck *their economic future.* Then perhaps America's youth will initiate an honest and informed dialogue with their parents and grandparents.

Ideally, what is needed are youth groups large enough and active enough to counteract the massive senior lobbies. That is why I enthusiastically support the young citizens' organization, Third Millennium, which already has members in every state—and which supplies speakers for college and corporate groups, testifies before Congress, and conducts research on generational issues.

The pessimists say, "Forget it." Americans will not reform senior benefits until a severe crisis is upon us but will persist in viewing them as contractual obligations which are by definition always affordable. After all, they say, an America that acknowledges limits is an America that has lost the one illu-

sion that makes it unique and creative. According to this view, America must always be an unteachable force of nature, living outside history, one that never reconsiders its promises or expectations no matter how excessive they have become. This, say the pessimists, is why American voters repeatedly elect leaders who promise lower taxes, higher benefits, rejuvenated economic growth, and a cure for every social problem—without caring how any of the pieces fit together.

My optimism that Americans will join together in raising our savings rates, balancing the budget, and reforming our entitlement programs is not glib Pollyannaism. I understand the difficulties. After all, I have been railing about our budgetary failings for nearly a quarter of a century. Still, I have seen more hopeful signs in the last few years than in the previous twenty.

When my first article on the need to reform Social Security appeared in 1982 in *The New York Review of Books,* the response was so hostile that the editors decided to devote a whole second issue to the controversy. It was called "Social Security: The Great Debate—Peter G. Peterson Replies to Critics." Most of the criticism challenged the idea that Social Security was in trouble or needed to be re-thought. Today, while the "don't worry—be happy" constituency is still strong, the vast majority of careful public-policy thinkers, whether liberal or conservative, have begun to debate the kinds of reform that are necessary, not whether or not basic reform is needed. Indeed, the last year alone has seen several major reform proposals put on the table by think tanks, presidential commissions, and even a few politicians—Democratic as well as Republican.

We also seem ready to talk seriously about the deficit and the importance of a balanced budget. Even many of my Republican friends considered me a "carper," as one once put it, when I stressed the need to restrain the deficit in the early 1980s. But no more. The issue has now moved from the outer

political margins to front and center in discussions between the White House and the Congress.

After an admirable start on deficit reduction in his first two years, President Clinton temporarily regressed to a plan that would have perpetuated $200-billion-a-year deficits. Under Republican pressure, he then agreed on the need to balance the budget but insisted on taking ten years to do so (and on using somewhat "soft" White House–backed Office of Management and Budget numbers). Then he agreed on seven years (using the more rigorous Congressional Budget Office numbers). It's been a long trip—with miles still to go. All too many of the current proposals to balance the budget by 2002 are disingenuous insofar as they are front loaded where tax cuts are concerned and shamelessly back loaded when it comes to spending cuts. And all, without exception, would allow the deficit to surge again after 2002. Nevertheless, there is now unprecedented bipartisan agreement that the budget *should* be balanced.

Along this politically difficult road, one must expect two steps forward and one back and a lot of partisan demagoguery in between. Bill Clinton denounced a "huge" Republican Medicare premium increase that would have required seniors to contribute a mere $4.80 a month more toward the cost of their insurance than the President's own plan, submitted only months earlier. Instead of working with the Republican leadership to reform a system that both parties know is on the verge of bankruptcy, the President sought to demonize the Republicans as "granny bashers"—even though the President's own plan two years before would have cut Medicare even more.[10]

As for the Republicans, we saw in the 1996 primary election campaign some new "rosy scenarios" concerning flat taxes and major tax cuts, as well as various other Reaganisms. Indeed, in the run-up to the New Hampshire primary in February 1996, the intra-Republican-party debate had so de-

parted from fiscal fundamentals that a front-page headline in *The New York Times* declared, DEFICIT ISSUE EVAPORATES. At that moment in the campaign, two rising Republican hopefuls, Steve Forbes and Pat Buchanan, were, according to the *Times,* unified only in the belief that the deficit is akin to the "dirty remnants of a big snowstorm—an eyesore that will melt away once the country changes its economic climate." Still, based on my own experience, I believe that Senator Bob Dole, Speaker Newt Gingrich, and other mainstream Republicans have never been more convinced of the need to build tomorrow's growth and opportunity on the foundation of a balanced budget and sustainable fiscal policies.

I also believe this is a propitious time for private citizens to step forward and take a leadership role. If someone with genuine moral authority but without all the partisan baggage were to speak out forcefully on these issues, that person could make a real difference. Warren Buffet tells me that the first name that comes to his mind is Colin Powell. I am sure Warren Buffet is right. A Colin Powell could make a big difference.

As a new Presidential election approaches, Americans can hope that the two major-party candidates, after asking themselves a few searching questions, will at last show some real leadership themselves.

The incumbent, Bill Clinton, is a lifetime policy wonk. Of all of today's political leaders, he will never be able to claim, later on, that he didn't know about America's savings dearth, the coming age wave, and the projected surge in old-age dependency costs. If he wins his second term, he will doubtless begin by looking forward to his legacy—to what people will be saying about his achievements a decade after his term expires, when he'll still be (in his mid-60s) a relatively youthful ex-President. How will he respond when people ask him: Where were you when we could have done something in ad-

vance about the age wave now crashing over us? You didn't *know* about it? Born in the first year (1946) of the postwar Baby Boom, Clinton's personal connection to the demographic problem will make any failure to act even harder to live down—especially among his own peers.

History often remembers presidents by a few memorable policy decisions—often, ironically, when they ran against the grain of their political stereotypes. Thus, Eisenhower, the military man, was uniquely able to warn against the dangers of the military-industrial complex. And Nixon, the anti-Communist hawk, was able to set in motion normal relations with China. The aging challenge, which involves all generations of Americans but the Baby Boom most of all, affords Bill Clinton a unique opportunity to make choices that will weigh heavily in all future evaluations of his presidency. Indeed, I have no doubt that his place in history will be greatly enhanced if he is remembered as the leader who called on his generation—and others—to face up to this great national challenge.

The challenger, Bob Dole, is a statesman who built a political career—and now a campaign identity—as a member of the World War II generation whose selfless valor once saved and rebuilt America. If he wins, he will also be asking himself about his legacy, albeit from a different perspective: Will the last President of this titanic generation of political leaders be known as the one who revived their "ask not" reputation for civic virtue? Or will he preside over the fire sale of their own youthful sacrifice? Dole will possess one unique advantage. No other contender will be able to talk as straight with senior citizens about the need to forge a consensus around some sacrifice from all generations.

Of course, given the realities of American politics, even those political leaders most seriously committed to a balanced budget may shy away from tough choices and take refuge in

disingenuous rhetoric, blaming the deficit, for example, on "welfare cheats" or "foreign aid"—when politicians in both parties know that these expenditures account for only a small fraction of the deficit while the real problem is ourselves and the huge river of entitlements that flows to the broad middle class. Politicians are not kamikaze pilots. They won't tell us the hard truths until the public makes it safer for them to do so. But on this front too, there is progress.

For example, the Business Roundtable, an umbrella organization of CEOs of major corporations, recently sponsored a multimillion-dollar public service TV and radio advertising campaign to raise public awareness about the long-term economic damage caused by chronic deficits. In a similar vein, when the White House and Capitol Hill came to a standstill over the balanced budget debate in the winter of 1995–96, some Republican and Democratic leaders asked me to rally CEOs of America's leading businesses to help break the impasse. In forty-eight hours, more than 120 CEOs agreed to sign a prominent two-page advertisement urging the President and the congressional leadership to seize the historic opportunity at hand. (The ad is reproduced on page 213) Leaders of both parties felt that this statement contributed to the bipartisan consensus that ultimately developed around balancing the budget in seven years based on the sterner Congressional Budget Office numbers. But what impressed me most was the alacrity with which the most senior figures in American business came forward to take a public stand on this issue.

My own efforts have been focused largely on the work of The Concord Coalition, the citizens' grassroots organization I founded in 1992 together with two of the most respected figures in contemporary American political life, former Senator Warren Rudman (a Republican) and former Senator Paul Tsongas (a Democrat). Other economic and fiscal pa-

triots who have joined our board of directors include former Fed Chairman Paul Volcker, former Congressman Tim Penny, former Senator Jack Danforth, and the late Barbara Jordan.

The Concord Coalition is devoted to educating the American public about the dangers of debts and deficits and to bringing about the change in national thinking that will make it safer for politicians to act. This "special interest" in behalf of the general interest and the future has thus far attracted nearly two hundred thousand members and has chapters in every state of the Union. When Concord speaks, leaders across the political spectrum listen. Virtually all Washington legislators are now aware of the Concord Debt Clock, its Zero Deficit Plan, its Debt Busters budget balancing exercises, its Facing Facts media alerts on entitlements, its Questions Voters Should Ask Their Candidates, and its Congressional Score Card on critical fiscal votes.

I have cited The Concord Coalition's experiences to show that the needed changes are possible and that, to some degree, they are already happening. But Concord, of course, is only one force among many that must come together if we are to transform American politics and implement a reform program like the one I have outlined in this book. Many groups in our society have broad and longer term interests that are being crowded out by the senior entitlements Pac-Man—scientists concerned about dwindling funding for basic research, teachers concerned about the deteriorating state of U.S. education, environmentalists concerned about the environment, internationalists who believe that America still has an "exceptional" role to play in world affairs. Unlike the benefit lobbies, these groups are not generally looking to advance their own narrow self-interest. They all need to become part of a new coalition, a "special interest" in behalf of the general interest.

My optimism is also based on my experiences in addressing audiences of all ages all over America. Indeed, I have hope—and lots of it—even for the supposedly "greedy geezers" of my own generation. In 1994, I was interviewed by *60 Minutes* on the need to enact gradual but far-reaching structural reforms of federal entitlements to the elderly. The network producers, after patiently taping my arguments, invited me to join them at a middle-class retirement community. Here, they said (with a few wry smiles), I could explain my suggestions to the people who would be most immediately affected.

Standing before this group of retired grandparents, I began by showing photographs of my own grandchildren. I explained my concerns about their future and the world they would inherit. I then reminded them how much of our own national affluence today rests on the willingness to make collective sacrifices they demonstrated during the Great Depression and World War II.

Sooner or later, I told them, we will have to prepare for a future challenge that we have so far ignored. We will have to balance our public budgets, reduce benefits to those who need them least, save more as households, retire somewhat later from the workforce, explore innovative means of economizing on health care, take a more effective public interest in the welfare of children, and offer the rising generation some tangible evidence that we are still willing to make sacrifices in their behalf. If we do so sooner, we can plan for a gradual and humane transformation. If we do so later, the changes are likely to be forced upon us, suddenly and painfully, in a crisis that may leave the eventual outcome much in doubt.

Given all that, I asked them: If everyone, young and old, is asked to sacrifice fairly to balance the budget, how many of you would agree to give up some share of your federal benefits, above what you need to live on, in order to ease the

deficit burden on younger generations? To the visible surprise of the *60 Minutes* producers, nearly all of them raised their hands.*

The generation I was speaking to survived the Depression . . . and fought and won World War II. After the war, this generation provided its returned veterans with college educations, built the interstate highway system, eradicated polio, took us to the moon, and won a cold war against communism. Against these monumental accomplishments, the steps to be taken now do not compare. I believe this generation can do the right thing and that politicians might well discover that it is better to appeal to their nobler instincts than pander to the baser ones.

A people who have grown used to quick gratification must now be asked to focus on the requirements of a society graced with the patina of age—on savings rather than consumption, on prudence rather than desire, on collective restraint rather than individual satisfaction. As Americans grow older, they must recognize that the live-for-today attitude that may be endearing or at least understandable in youth is not only unseemly but massively dysfunctional at the far end of life. They will do well to heed the eighteenth-century French moralist Joseph Joubert, who warned: "The passions of the young are vices in the old."

---

* I was surprised myself by this response. I asked how many were members of the American Association of Retired Persons. Virtually all raised their hands. How, then, I asked, could card-carrying members of the AARP support a program like mine. Two gentlemen leapt to their feet. Both said, in effect, "Oh, the AARP doesn't represent us with their policy positions. Basically, we are members because of the discounts we get—travel, insurance, prescriptions and the like." I looked around the room and virtually all were nodding affirmatively.

11

Which Future?

There are moments in the history of great nations when a single choice can mean the difference between alternative futures—one bright, the other dark.

Imagine what America might be like if we could simply achieve the productivity growth rate—1.5 percent, or an extra 1 percentage point per year—to which I have referred. The target is modest—our growth rate would still be lower than that of most other industrial nations—but the results would be mighty. The typical full-time American worker now annually produces about $38,000 in national income—an amount that has hardly budged over the past twenty-five years. But if we change course and meet our modest productivity target, national income per worker would rise to $55,000 (in today's dollars) over the next twenty-five years, or by 45 percent. Once again, grown children could look back on their parents as relative paupers; and once again, parents could take pride in the opportunities they would be passing on to their children. Such a difference is the stuff the American Dream is made of.

Twenty-five years from now, our growth target would also translate into $490 billion annually in extra federal revenue (at today's prices and at unchanged tax rates).[1] This is enough to help ensure budget balance while still pursuing many social goals we now cannot afford. The public resources would once again be available for helping poor kids get a better start in life; for protecting the environment; for defending democracy abroad; for exploring space; and for tackling many of the other frontier issues of our time. The divergence in fortunes between old and young and rich and poor will narrow, and as in the past, a rapidly growing economy would benefit us all.

But there is also another future—a dark future in which we close our eyes to the inevitable and condemn our own posterity. This is the future in which an aging society, flattered by cheap talk about inevitable prosperity and the inviolability of entitlement programs, does nothing—and by doing nothing, grows old gracelessly and destructively.

By doing nothing—that is, by making no significant change in federal benefits or federal taxes—we would wreak the certain destruction of our economy well within the lifetime of most Baby Boomers. Inaction, according to a 1996 report of the General Accounting Office (GAO), would give rise by 2026 to federal deficits of roughly 25 percent of GDP, an amount that would vastly exceed not just the net savings of the United States but the total capital exports of all industrial nations. Such deficits are not merely unsustainable; they are not even attainable, for our economy would surely implode long before 2026. Almost pointlessly, the GAO adds that the study's "alarming" results are "probably understated," as though a 25-percent-of-GDP deficit were not a sufficiently chilling prospect. Then there is the further prospect of chaos in global capital markets. Remember: Other industrial countries confront unfunded retirement liabilities even larger and less sustainable than our own. Even if they take vigorous ac-

tion to reduce their liabilities, they may only be willing to export savings at high and rising interest rates.

Yes, we might try to muddle through by enacting just enough benefit cuts and tax hikes to keep the federal deficit from growing unmanageably. But unless benefits are radically reformed, this approach will, in time, translate primarily into ever higher tax hikes, which in turn will depress after-tax wages. At the same time, unless benefits are radically reformed, savings will be on a starvation diet, meaning that productivity and pre-tax wage growth will likely not even match their meager current trend. If we do nothing more than muddle through, most working families will probably suffer a long-term decline in their real disposable income and perhaps recall nostalgically the mere stagnation of the 1980s and 1990s.

The same psychology of denial that sustains our present system also increases the risk that financial markets will march off a cliff. This could happen as soon as 2005, when first-born Boomers start withdrawing funds from their 401(k)s and Keoghs. Or in 2011, when they reach age sixty-five. Or in 2013, when Social Security is projected to run its first cash deficit. As all financial analysts are aware, it's never easy to predict the timing of the market's response to economic and fiscal developments, even if its ultimate destination is perfectly clear.

The same entitlement ethos that says that your future benefit is akin to a property right—even if you're rich enough not to need it—may eventually spawn a new generation of young people who will organize their own junior citizens' clubs and vote their elders down. And when they do, they may not care much about abrupt cutbacks or whether the elders who lose their benefits include those who really do need them. Today's youngsters grow up hearing their parents and leaders constantly proclaim the urgent morality of acting in behalf of our young people. Ten or twenty years from now, when these

young people of Generations Y and Z are in college, won't they perhaps decide, as a group, that the time has come for their elders to practice what they've been preaching? Will they find, as today's elders did in their own youth during the 1930s, an FDR-like champion who favors reshuffling the economic deck to the detriment of old creditors and the benefit of young workers? And then what? What will be the reaction of Boomers, the elders of the 2020s, when they come face-to-face with large, sudden cuts in Social Security or draconian rationing of public health-care benefits? Will they break all life cycle precedent and suffer this blow with obliging good humor—or will their last political act (like their first) be to throw the nation into turmoil?

Above all, the same dynamic of social unraveling that prevents Americans from achieving any consensus may over time turn into a genuine and dangerous fragmentation of our national polity. The American Dream of material progress, from one generation to the next, is not just the result of social discipline; it is also its cause. Precisely because Americans have historically shared a reasonable hope in a bright future, they have been able to join in overcoming differences of class, race, income, and region that might paralyze another society. If nothing else, a faith in progress encourages the hope that a social injustice, if uncorrected in this generation, will be corrected in the next.

This social dynamic will be thrown into reverse if America does not face up promptly to the costs of its own aging. Low-income wage earners will soon start asking why they're paying for the amenities of affluent retirees; immigrants who send money back home to their parents will ask why they must also support elder Anglos; residents of Utah and Louisiana will ask why they are paying for nursing homes in New York and Minnesota. All Americans will wonder why they're getting such a bad deal from a system of old-age security which, in the end, can no longer deliver at all on what the

system's defenders have always claimed to be its paramount advantage—namely, *security.*

The "crowding out" concept that has a clear financial meaning (to siphon private savings from private investment) also has a clear fiscal meaning (to squeeze public-purpose spending out of public-purpose budgets). What we may soon find is that "crowding out" may also have a long-term social meaning. No one knows what American society might be like once it has fully accepted static living standards as a permanent way of life. But it is easy to imagine that our society will be far less generous and less hopeful, and far more fearful and angry, than what we are used to, a society with far less to spare for anything more than getting by.

So we must do more than hope. We must plan now to redirect ourselves toward the goal we all desire: a future worth preparing for. We have no choice. Only time will tell if we have the courage. Or as George Stigler, my Nobel Prize–winning professor at the University of Chicago, used to put it, "If you have no alternative, you have no problem." We don't have an alternative, which is to say, the only real problem we face is ourselves.

A Bipartisan Appeal from Business Leaders
to the President of the United States Bill Clinton,
House Speaker Newt Gingrich, Senate Majority Leader Bob Dole,
Senate Minority Leader Tom Daschle, House Majority Leader Dick Armey,
House Minority Leader Dick Gephardt, and All Members of Congress:

WITHOUT A BALANCED BUDGET, THE PARTY'S OVER. NO MATTER WHICH PARTY YOU'RE IN.

There are moments in history when a single choice can mean the difference between vastly differing futures — one bright, the other dark. We believe that you, the political leaders of this country, are now confronting such a choice in your deliberations over a plan to balance the federal budget.

We are convinced that the health of our economy rests on your ability to avoid political gridlock and give the American people what leaders of both parties say they favor and, indeed, have agreed to — a credible plan to balance the budget. By "credible" we mean that such a plan should:

- Use realistic projections that assume the fiscal and economic scenario developed by the Congressional Budget Office and reviewed by objective third parties;

- Take no longer than seven years as the maximum time period by which a balanced budget would be achieved;

- Ensure that the process of deficit reduction is achieved in roughly equal steps throughout these seven years, rather than "backloading" the politically difficult decisions into the next century; and

- Have everything on the table, including long-term entitlement programs as well as the size and shape of any tax cuts.

Included among us are Democrats and Republicans, Liberals and Conservatives. What unites us in this appeal is our common concern for America's future.

All of us are leaders of institutions keenly sensitive to interest rates and the short- and long-term outlook for the U.S. economy. We believe that the recent decline in long-term interest rates and much of the boom in the stock market is directly predicated on the financial markets' expectation that a successful bipartisan budget-balancing compromise will be reached quickly, and that a credible long-term plan will be put in place in short order.

Federal Reserve Board Chairman Alan Greenspan recently observed: "If there is a shattering of expectations that leads to the conclusion that there is indeed an inability to ultimately redress the corrosive forces of deficit, I think the reaction would be quite negative — that is, a sharp increase in long-term interest rates... I think we would find that with mortgage rates higher and other related rates moving up, interest-sensitive areas of the economy would begin to run into trouble."

As you continue your negotiations, we ask you to reflect on the full consequences of success or failure. However Americans ultimately resolve our honest and principled disagreements over the size and scope of government, America must begin to live within its means.

The time for good economics as well as good politics is NOW.

America is waiting.

Respectfully yours,

Paul Allaire	Jon Corzine	M.R. Greenberg
Chairman and CEO	Chairman and Senior Partner	Chairman and CEO
Xerox Corporation	Goldman, Sachs & Co.	American International Group, Inc.
Richard H. Jenrette	Peter G. Peterson	John Snow
Chairman and CEO	Chairman, The Blackstone Group	Chairman and CEO, CSX Corporation
The Equitable Companies, Incorporated	President, The Concord Coalition	Chairman, The Business Roundtable

This message has been paid for by the above named individuals and organizations.

Notes

1. "A Nation of Floridas"

1. This book is filled with demographic projections. With a few exceptions, the projections I use are the 1995 "Social Security Area Population Projections" prepared by the Office of the Actuary of the Social Security Administration (SSA). The basic numbers are published in the 1995 *Annual Report of the Board of Trustees of the Federal Old-Age and Survivors Insurance and Disability Insurance Trust Funds;* some of the more detailed numbers are drawn from unpublished data supplied by the Office of the Actuary. As a rule, the numbers I cite refer to SSA's "intermediate" scenario, the benchmark used by most demographers, economists, and policymakers. This is a fiscally optimistic scenario that assumes modest gains in longevity, buoyant fertility rates, and high levels of net immigration. To give an idea of what our demographic future will look like if this "optimism" proves unfounded, I occasionally cite SSA's more prudent "high-cost" scenario.

2. This number is the combined unfunded benefit liability (at the end of fiscal year 1995) of the four major entitlement programs for which figures are available: civil service and military pensions, Social Security, and Medicare. The figures for federal pensions (a total of $1.5 trillion) are published in the *Budget of the United States Government: FY 1996.* The figure for Social Security ($8 trillion) was supplied by the

SSA's Office of the Actuary; the figure for Medicare ($7.3 trillion) is based on calculations in A. Haeworth Robertson, *Social Security: What Every Taxpayer Should Know* (Retirement Policy Institute, 1992). These numbers do not offset liabilities by current trust-fund "assets," since such intragovernmental obligations do not represent true funding. If we counted them as assets to individual benefit programs we would have to turn around and count them as liabilities to the Treasury. The net effect on the federal government's balance sheet would be zero.

2. Demographics Is Destiny

1. The demographic projections that follow come from the Social Security Administration's Office of the Actuary. (See note 1 above.) The one exception is for population by race, where I have used Census Bureau projections (SSA does not project race). See *Population Projections of the United States, by Age, Sex, and Hispanic Origin: 1993 to 2050,"* Current Population Reports, series P25, no. 1104 (Bureau of the Census, 1993).
2. These figures are calculated by actuaries at the Health Care Financing Administration, which administers Medicare and Medicaid. See Daniel Waldo et al., "Health Expenditures by Age Group, 1977 and 1987," *Health Care Financing Review* (Summer 1989).
3. Cited in "New Views on Life Spans Alter Forecasts on Elderly," *The New York Times* (November 16, 1992).
4. My discussion of foreign retirement systems draws on numerous articles and studies, but especially the superb 1994 World Bank report *Averting the Old Age Crisis: Policies to Protect the Old and Promote Growth*.
5. For the 1986 communiqué, see Peter G. Peterson and Neil Howe, *On Borrowed Time: How the Growth in Entitlement Spending Threatens America's Future* (Institute for Contemporary Studies, 1988), pp. 21–23. The remarks of Prime Minister Hashimoto are quoted in two January 1996 press releases obtained from the Japan Information Center.

3. Unsustainable Promises

1. All projections of Social Security and Medicare cash deficits refer to the SSA's official intermediate scenario. See the *1995 Annual Report of the Board of Trustees of the Federal Old-Age and Survivors Insurance and Disability Insurance Trust Funds*.
2. All payroll cost projections are from the *1995 Annual Report of the Board of Trustees of the Federal Old-Age and Survivors Insurance and Disability Insurance Trust Funds* and the *1995 Annual Report of*

the Board of Trustees of the Federal Hospital Insurance Trust Fund. Although Medicare Supplementary Medical Insurance (SMI) is not payroll-tax financed, SMI costs are expressed as a share of payroll to allow consistent projection of total Social Security and Medicare costs. The government actuaries do not prepare a "high-cost" SMI projection; this was derived by assuming that SMI cost rates will exceed SMI cost rates in the intermediate scenario by the same proportion as cost rates in the Medicare Hospital Insurance (HI) high-cost scenario exceed those in the intermediate HI scenario.

3. The projections of total benefit outlays and real after-tax wages cited here and immediately below are all directly derived from the SSA's (1994) economic and demographic scenarios. See Neil Howe, *Why the Graying of the Welfare State Threatens to Flatten the American Dream—or Worse* (National Taxpayers Union Foundation, 1994).

4. Data for AFDC are from the *1994 Green Book* (House Ways and Means Committee, 1994); data for Social Security are from the *1995 Annual Report of the Board of Trustees of the Federal Old-Age and Survivors Insurance and Disability Insurance Trust Funds.*

5. See *1994 Green Book.*

6. All Social Security and Medicare "paybacks" are calculated as present value figures at age sixty-five using a 2 percent real interest rate. See Eugene Steuerle, *Retooling Social Security for the 21st Century* (Urban Institute, 1994).

7. The sources for federal benefit liabilities at the end of FY 1995 are cited in note 2 to chapter 1 above. These calculations assume that benefit liabilities are amortized over thirty years, the rule that is enforced for private pension plans under the Employee Retirement Income Security Act.

8. See *1994 Green Book* and *Reducing Entitlement Spending* (CBO, 1994).

4. The Inescapable Bottom Line

1. Paul Krugman, *The Age of Diminished Expectations: U.S. Economic Policy in the 1990s* (MIT Press, 1990), p. 9.

2. U.S. data on per-worker national income, compensation, and wages are from the Commerce Department's National Income and Product Accounts (NIPA) and are published periodically in the Commerce Department's *Survey of Current Business.* Basic economic data for other industrial countries (including the productivity and savings and investment rates cited later in the chapter) are from the Organisation for Economic Co-operation and Development's latest *National Accounts* and *OECD Economic Outlook.*

3. Private-sector savings is the sum of household or personal savings and business savings; net national savings is private savings plus or minus the public-sector surplus or deficit. Unless otherwise indicated, all data on U.S. savings and investment in this book are from the Commerce Department's National Income and Product Accounts. (See note 2 above.)

4. See Craig S. Karpel, *The Retirement Myth* (Harper-Collins, 1995), pp. 81–95; and Sylvester J. Schieber and John B. Shoven, "The Consequences of Population Aging on Private Pension Fund Saving and Asset Markets," in *The Economics of U.S. Retirement Policy: Current Status and Future Directions*, ed. Sylvester J. Schieber and John B. Shoven (Twentieth Century Fund, 1996).

5. Francis Walker, "The National Debt," cited in Robert T. Paterson, *Federal Debt Management Policies, 1865–1879* (Duke University Press, 1954), p. 56.

6. Data on federal investment spending are from the *Fiscal Year 1996 Budget of the United States Government* (Office of Management and Budget, 1995). Outlay figures for discretionary spending are from *The Economic and Budget: Fiscal Years 1996–2000* (CBO, 1995).

7. For the House budget resolution, see *Concurrent Resolution on the Budget for Fiscal Year 1996* (U.S. House of Representatives, May 1995); for the administration's January budget proposal, see "Tweedledum and Tweedledee," *Facing Facts*, 2:1 (The Concord Coalition; January 19, 1996).

8. As defined here, senior benefits are strictly benefits to persons age sixty-five and over. If we included Social Security and federal pension benefits to persons under age sixty-five, the numbers would be even more dramatic. All calculations are from "Seniors Will Still Get More—Under Any Budget Plan," *Facing Facts*, 1:2 (The Concord Coalition; June 16, 1995).

9. *School Facilities: Condition of America's Schools* (General Accounting Office, 1995).

10. This startling conclusion was one of the central findings of the Bipartisan Commission on Entitlement and Tax Reform on which I served. See the *Interim Report to the President of the Bipartisan Commission on Entitlement and Tax Reform* (1994).

5. America's Savings Gap

1. My discussion of retirement attitudes draws on polling data cited in the following studies and surveys: *Saving the American Dream: An Economic and Public Opinion Study* (Merrill Lynch, 1994); *Who Will Pay for Your Retirement? The Looming Crisis* (Committee for Economic

Development, 1995); *Promises to Keep: How Leaders and the Public Respond to Saving and Retirement* (Public Agenda, 1994); and the *Survey on Retirement Confidence,* started by the National Taxpayers Union Foundation and now conducted yearly by the Employee Benefit Research Institute.

2. For the statistics on pension coverage, see *Trends in Pensions 1992* (U.S. Department of Labor, 1992). For the typical defined-benefit replacement rate, see *Employee Benefits in Medium and Large Private Establishments 1991* (U.S. Department of Labor, 1993).

3. The Federal Reserve Board data are cited in "How Not to Think About the Savings Rate" (Peter L. Bernstein, Inc.; July 15, 1995). For the analysis of Census Bureau data, see Joseph M. Anderson, *The Wealth of U.S. Families in 1991 and 1993* (Merrill Lynch, 1994).

4. See B. Douglas Bernheim, *The Merrill Lynch Baby Boom Retirement Index* (Merrill Lynch, 1994).

5. See the *1994 Survey on Entitlements,* conducted by the National Taxpayers Union Foundation and the Congressional Institute for the Future.

6. See *Promises to Keep.*

7. See Brian O'Reilly, "Busted Boomers: Here's the Wake-Up Call," *Fortune* (July 24, 1995).

6. From the World's Biggest Saver to the World's Biggest Consumer

1. Cited in Sylvia Ann Hewlett, *When the Bow Breaks: The Cost of Neglecting our Children* (Basic Books, 1991), pp. 78–79.

2. *Newsweek* (February 13, 1967).

3. Cited in an interview with Joseph A. Califano, Jr., President Carter's Secretary of Health, Education, and Welfare. "Califano Recalls Earlier Health Reform Battles," *Washington Post Health* (September 21, 1993).

4. President's message to Congress, June 8, 1934.

5. Daniel Bell, *The Cultural Contradictions of Capitalism* (Basic Books, 1976), p. 233.

6. Historical numbers are my estimates based on legislated COLAs and annual outlays for indexed entitlement programs. My five-year projection is derived from similar projections published by the Congressional Budget Office. See *Reducing the Deficit: Spending and Revenue Options* (CBO, 1995).

7. Formally designated the President's Private Sector Survey on Cost Control, the Commission is commonly called the Grace Commission after its chairman, W. R. Grace. See *President's Private Sector Survey on Cost Control: A Report to the President* (1984).

8. All quotations in the following discussion of the Reagan tax cut are from David Stockman, *The Triumph of Politics: Why the Reagan Revolution Failed* (Harper & Row, 1986).

7. America's Denial Syndrome

1. For financial wealth, see *Household Wealth and Asset Ownership: 1991,* Current Population Reports, Series P-70, no. 34 (Bureau of the Census, 1994). For income and poverty, see *Measuring the Effect of Benefits and Taxes on Income and Poverty: 1992,* Current Population Reports, Series P-60, no. 186-RD (Bureau of the Census, 1993). For consumption rates, see Jagadeesh Gokhale, Laurence Kotlikoff, and John Sabelhaus, *Understanding the Postwar Decline in United States Saving: A Cohort Analysis,* (National Bureau of Economic Research, 1994).

2. These shares refer to benefits going to households with incomes above $30,000 in 1990, approximately the U.S. median income that year. See *Reducing Entitlement Spending* (CBO, 1994).

3. See *Social Security: Universal or Selective. A Debate between Milton Friedman and Wilbur J. Cohen* (American Enterprise Institute, 1972).

4. Mancur Olsen, "Ideology and Economic Growth," in *The Legacy of Reaganomics: Prospects for Long-Term Growth,* ed. Charles R. Hamiltion and Isabel V. Sawhill (Urban Institute, 1984).

5. The data, which are from the Congressional Budget Office and the Joint Committee on Taxation, are published in Neil Howe, *How to Control the Growth of Federal Entitlements: The Argument for Comprehensive "Means-Testing"* (National Taxpayers Union Foundation, 1991).

6. *1993 Green Book* (House Ways and Means Committee, 1993).

7. The definition of income used here is "expanded family income," which differs somewhat from the standard Census Bureau cash income concept. Income distributions were calculated by Pete Davis (President of Davis Capital Investment Ideas) based on data supplied by KPMG Peat Marwick.

8. Praying for Productivity and Other Good Things

1. Richard Leone, "Don't Worry, Generation X," *The Washington Post* (April 30, 1996).

2. "Listen Up, Generation X," *Facing Facts,* 2:5 (The Concord Coalition; May 2, 1996).

3. For the sensitivity analysis cited here (as well as in the following discussion of immigration and health-care costs), see Richard Jackson, "The Inevitability of Entitlement Reform: An Analysis of the Social Security and Medicare Long-Term Cost Projections," in the *Final Report*

to the President of the Bipartisan Commission on Entitlement and Tax Reform (1995).

9. Seven Coming Transformations

1. See *Saving for Our Future* (Australian Government Publishing Service, 1995).
2. For Singapore, see the *1994 CPF Annual Report* (Central Provident Fund Board, 1994) and *The CPF Story* (Central Provident Fund Board, 1995). Among the large and growing number of studies on the Chilean reform, I found the following especially useful: *The Chilean Private Pension System* (The International Center for Pension Reform, 1995); Peter Diamond and Salvador Valdés-Prieto, "Social Security Reforms," in *The Chilean Economy: Policy Lessons and Challenges,* ed. Barry Bosworth et al. (The Brookings Institution, 1995); and Peter Ferrara et al., *Private Alternatives to Social Security in Other Countries* (National Center for Policy Analysis, 1995).
3. José Penera, *Empowering Workers: The Privatization of Social Security in Chile* (Cato Institute, 1986).
4. Cited in Craig Karpel, *The Retirement Myth,* p. 101.
5. Figures for per capita health-benefit spending on the elderly in 1965 and 1975 are from Charles Fisher, "Differences by Age Groups in Health Care Spending," *Health Care Financing Review* (Spring 1980); the figure for 1995 is estimated on the basis of age-specific spending data in Daniel Waldo et al., "Health Expenditures by Age Group, 1977 and 1987"; the figure for the eve of the New Deal (1935) is estimated on the basis of NIPA data. Data on total U.S. health-care spending (both historical and projected) are from the Health Care Financing Administration's National Health Accounts and are published periodically in the *Health Care Financing Review.* Data on per capita health-care expenditures in other industrial countries are from George Schieber et al., "Health Spending, Delivery, and Outcomes in OECD Countries," *Health Affairs* (Summer 1993).
6. See J. Lubitz and R. Prihoda, "The Use of and Costs of Medicare Services in the Last Two Years of Life," *Health Care Financing Review* (1985).
7. Excerpted from a letter from Fred Plum published in my book *Facing Up: Paying Our Nation's Debt and Saving Our Children's Future* (Simon & Schuster, 1994), pp. 150–53.
8. For incomes, see *Money Income of Households, Families, and Persons in the United States: 1992,* Current Population Reports, Series P-60, no. 184 (Bureau of the Census, 1993). For poverty rates, see *Measuring the Effect of Benefits and Taxes on Income and Poverty: 1992.*
9. This ratio is based on data on entitlement benefits published in the *1993 Green Book.* If we add in federal nonentitlement outlays specifi-

cally targeted at children and the elderly, the ratio is somewhat lower—eleven to one in 1990. See Neil Howe and Richard Jackson, *Entitlements and the Aging of America* (National Taxpayers Union Foundation, 1994), chart 3-4.

10. Assumed age-specific voting rates in this projection are averages for the 1990 and 1992 elections; population by age group in 2040 is from the SSA's (1994) intermediate scenario.

11. See Paul Van den Noord and Richard Herd, *Pension Liabilities in the Seven Major Economies*, Working Paper 142 (OECD, 1993).

10. Turning America from Consumption and Deficits to Savings and Investment: What Needs to Be Done

1. All savings figures in the text and accompanying charts are calculated against outlays under the SSA's intermediate scenario. For the affluence test and the retirement age hike, the savings refer to the reforms specified later in this chapter. The savings from benefit taxation are the savings that would be achieved by taxing 85 percent of Social Security benefits (with no income thresholds). The fiscal effect of this reform is roughly equivalent to full taxation of Social Security benefits under the consumed income tax system I propose below.

2. See "Reform Proposal of Commissioner Peter G. Peterson," in the *Final Report to the President of the Bipartisan Commission on Entitlement and Tax Reform.*

3. See *Public Opinion Toward Entitlements and the Federal Deficit: A National Voter Survey* (The Concord Coalition, 1995).

4. See *Reducing the Deficit: Spending and Revenue Options.*

5. See "It's Time to Say No to Medicaid for the Middle Class," *Facing Facts*, 2:2 (The Concord Coalition; February 19, 1996).

6. For the $5 billion annual budget cost of repealing the earnings test, see the *1993 Green Book*. This figure takes into account neither offsetting benefit reductions under an affluence test nor possible additions to federal income tax revenue due to increased employment. The net cost of repealing the earnings test would thus be significantly less.

7. See, for instance, *Older Workers are Good Investments: A Case Study of Days Inns of America's Reservation Center* (The Commonwealth Fund, 1991).

8. See *National Thrift Plan Project: Interim Report,* prepared by Neil Howe and Richard Jackson (National Taxpayers Union Foundation and the Center For Public Policy and Contemporary Issues, March 1996).

9. See *Estimates for a Prototype Saving-Exempt Income Tax* (CBO, March 1994).

10. See "A Budget Train Wreck—All Over $4.80 a Month in Medicare Premiums," *Facing Facts,* 1:11 (The Concord Coalition; November 14, 1995) and "The Forgotten Numbers in the Medicare Debate," *Facing Facts,* 1:5 (The Concord Coaliton; August 6, 1995).

11. Which Future?

1. This extra revenue is the fiscal dividend that would result if per-worker national income were to grow at 1.5 percent per year instead of its post-1973 average of 0.4 percent per year.

Index

Aaron, Henry, 139–40
affluence tests, *see* means tests
Affluent Society, The (Galbraith),
  89
age-wave transformation, *see*
  demographic transformation
aggregate personal savings rate,
  75
Aid to Families with Dependent
  Children (AFDC), 40
American Association of Retired
  Persons (AARP), 27, 28,
  111–12, 148
American Dream, 3, 5, 38, 51,
  53, 67, 123–24, 211
American High, 5–6
American Hospital Association,
  94
American Medical Association
  (AMA), 94
annual consolidated budget
  deficit (surplus), 48
apprenticeship programs, 147

Argentina, funded retirement
  system in, 30
asset prices, in retirement planning, 61
atomic weapons, 82, 85
Australia, and mandatory
  employer pensions, 27,
  131–32, 134, 196
Averting the Old Age Crisis
  (World Bank), 181

Baby Boom generation
  aging of, 3, 9, 15
  impact of, 13
  and inheritance, 76–77
  Peter Pan culture of, 20
  retirement planning and,
    73–80
  saving by, 74–76
  see also demographic transfor-
    mation
balanced budget, 17, 113,
  155–61, 188, 200–4, 209

ABOUT THE AUTHOR

PETER G. PETERSON is Chairman of The Blackstone Group, Director of the Federal Reserve Bank of New York, Chairman of the Council on Foreign Relations, Chairman of the Institute for International Economies, and Founding President of The Concord Coalition. In 1994, he was appointed by President Clinton to the Bipartisan Commission on Entitlement and Tax Reform. Mr. Peterson has received countless awards, including the National Magazine Award for the Best Public Interest Article of the Year in 1987.

ABOUT THE TYPE

This book was set in Sabon, a typeface designed by the well-known German typographer Jan Tschichold (1902–74). Sabon's design is based upon the original letter forms of Claude Garamond and was created specifically to be used for three sources: foundry type for hand composition, Linotype, and Monotype. Tschichold named his typeface for the famous Frankfurt typefounder Jacques Sabon, who died in 1580.